CHICANISMO

CHICANISMO

The Forging of a Militant Ethos
among Mexican Americans

Ignacio M. García

The University of Arizona Press   Tucson

The University of Arizona Press
© 1997 Arizona Board of Regents
All rights reserved

02 01 00   6 5 4 3

Library of Congress Cataloging-in-Publication Data
García, Ignacio M.
Chicanismo : the forging of a militant ethos among Mexican
Americans / Ignacio M. García.
p. cm.
Includes bibliographical references (p.) and index.
ISBN 0-8165-1787-8 (cloth : acid-free paper). —
ISBN 0-8165-1788-6 (pbk. : acid-free paper)
1. Mexican Americans—Politics and government.   2. Mexican
Americans—Ethnic identity.   I. Title.
E184.M5G365   1997
320.54′089′6872087—dc21   97-4815
CIP

British Library Cataloguing-in-Publication Data
A catalogue record for this book is available from
the British Library.

This book is dedicated to my father, mother, and brother. My father, because his funny stories of political activism in Mexico not only had us rolling on our backs but also stirred within me a profound interest in political activism. My mother, because her short plays for the barrio church we attended inspired my love for the written word. And my brother, because his love of books and his intense desire to accumulate knowledge taught me what it takes to be an intellectual. Together they helped me rise above my limitations. *Gracias, mi familia querida.*

Contents

Acknowledgments

A book is always the result of many minds and just as many hearts. I could not possibly acknowledge everyone who has been directly and indirectly connected with this project. There are, however, those for whom I have particular praise. I begin with two church youth leaders who first started me thinking about what it means to be a Mexican in American society. Refugio "Cuco" Jaime taught me that my ethnicity had a particular purpose, maybe even a divine one, and for that reason I must always be proud of who I am. Roberto Rodríguez instilled in me a sense of responsibility for my people and encouraged me to have passion in all I do. Without their encouragement and the spiritual values they taught me, I would never have pursued the course I did. I have never had a chance to thank them before. *Gracias.*

This manuscript has been reviewed by a number of people. Each one provided new ideas and helped me to discard old ones that led nowhere. Three scholars who read and reread the earlier drafts were Oscar J. Martínez, John A. García, and Juan R. García, all three members of the faculty at the University of Arizona. They were critical and at times unrelenting, but most of the time they were supportive. They challenged me to define and refine my analysis. Most of the best advice came during short telephone calls and from handwritten notes, but it served to keep me going. At Texas A & M University in Corpus Christi, I benefited greatly from the support of three wonderful colleagues. Patrick Carroll, Robert Wooster, and Alan Lessoff all read my manuscript and convinced me that it would see the light of day in the publishing world. Professor Lessoff was particularly helpful in reading my chapter on Robstown and providing insightful suggestions.

Another important individual in Corpus Christi was Paul L. Hain, dean of the College of Arts and Humanities, who lessened my teaching load and provided much-needed travel funds. From the college, I received a summer grant in 1994 that helped me finish most of my research. Another special person at Texas A & M was Judy McFerren, the department secretary, who did many things to lighten my load and keep me working on the book. The two years I spent in Corpus Christi were extremely valuable, and I will always have a special place in my heart for the "Island University."

Two other colleagues played a major part in the development of this work. Salomón Baldenegro, dean of Chicano/Hispanic Student Affairs at the University of Arizona, shared his personal documents from the Chicano Movement and his vivid recollection to help me better understand the minds of the Chicano activists of the 1960s and 1970s. And Roberto De Anda, assistant professor of sociology at the University of Illinois, Urbana-Champaign, was my intellectual mentor. We spent hours talking on the phone, and his poignant questions forced me to focus on what I was trying to prove. Finally, my wife, Alejandra, helped me to keep going when I was not sure that I would contribute anything new. Her personal analysis of the Chicano Movement helped me realize that the personal perspective would have to play a major role in this work. And my children, Roman, Veronica, Ignacio, and Valeria, always believed that their father had something to say. To all of them, *gracias*.

I could not end without thanking the University of Arizona Press staff for the wonderful job they have done. Susan Fansler did a wonderful job of editing and providing helpful suggestions. Especially worthy of thanks is Joanne O'Hare, who saw the worth of the manuscript. Her positive assessment came at an important time. Thank you, Joanne.

CHICANISMO

Introduction

Starting in the early 1960s and ending in the late 1970s, a large number of organizations and individuals appeared in Mexican American communities across the country, agitating for social and political change and promoting a militant version of self-help and racial solidarity. This social activism came to be known as the Chicano Movement, or Movimiento—the most traumatic and profound social movement ever to occur among Mexicans on the U.S. side of the Rio Grande. This movement caused a fundamental shift in the way Mexican Americans saw themselves, practiced their politics, and accommodated to American society. Elites arose who debated and discussed the issue of being Mexican in American society. This debate, and the subsequent change in attitude that it engendered, led to a number of new artistic and intellectual currents within the Mexican American community. Artists developed a form of art that extolled the virtues of the barrio and of the Mexican indigenous past; writers and poets created a literature that was bilingual, defiant, and working class oriented; and scholars and grassroots intellectuals developed a scholarship that created a new historical construct that freed Mexican Americans from self-victimization and shifted the blame for Mexican American powerlessness to Anglo-American society. All of these actions were spurred on by a politics of self-identity and communal empowerment that sought to transcend class and social barriers imposed from within and from outside the Mexican American community. A political "consciousness" of being *mexicano* in the United States gave rise to a militant ethos that became the impetus for this social upheaval. This ethos sought to synthesize the problems of the Mexican American community in terms that most Mexican Americans could understand and to which they could relate. It "spoke their language," a language buttressed by years of discrimination, violence, and neglect from the American mainstream. The ethos also promoted solutions to powerlessness and poverty that went much further than those of most other Chicano resistance movements, at least rhetorically and conceptually.[1]

When I use the term "militant ethos," I refer to that body of ideas, strategies, tactics, and rationalizations that a community uses to respond to external challenges. In this case, a Chicano militant ethos would be the collective defensive and offensive mechanism that the Mexican American community uses to combat racism, discrimination, poverty, and segregation, and to define itself politically and historically.[2] I argue that during the early 1960s and through the late 1970s, the Chicano community's activists, reformers, and intellectuals went through several stages in their philosophical evolution. During that process, the Movimiento arose and played itself out. This process proved to be uneven and, at times, unfocused and contradictory. Nevertheless it encompassed the multiplicity of ideas that prevailed in the Mexican American community. The Chicano Movement was not so much a singular social process as a coalescing of numerous philosophical and historical currents within the community that came together at a particular time and place during this century. The unification of these thoughts caused Mexican Americans to see themselves as a community with a past and a future.

A historical definition of the Chicano Movement and a review of what scholars have said about this social process are imperative before I set forth the steps of this process. The Chicano Movement may be defined as a social movement that emerged in the 1960s to protest the circumstances in which the Mexican American community found itself. This emotional, but predominantly nonviolent, reform movement included several concerns of great importance to a diverse community. Among these were the fear of cultural disintegration, the lack of economic and social mobility, rampant discrimination, and inadequate educational institutions. The Movement did not have an exclusively political or electoral character; Chicanos fought racism and neglect in education and housing and in the realm of culture and identity. Chicano pride became an important element of the Movement.[3] For many activists, the Mexican American community had reached a juncture in its historical odyssey that required a social and political outburst similar to those of women, African Americans, middle-class youth, and others who rebelled in the 1960s.

Rodolfo Acuña describes the Movement as a renewal of the ongoing struggle of Chicanos to liberate themselves from racism and exploitation. His analysis, once couched in the theory of "internal colonialism,"[4] presents the Chicano Movement as something that was not new or particularly different from the struggles of the past, with the exception that it was more national in scope and was waged predominantly in the urban areas. This urban context minimized the impact of the farmworkers' union in California and the land-grant battles in New Mexico. Though he abandoned his internal-colony model, Acuña continued to center his argument about Chicano oppression on the military conquest of the Southwest and its colonizing effects.[5] Even as new immigrants came into this country, they fell into the segmented circumstances created by the conquest and colonization. In Acuña's view, the 1960s were dominated by a search for causes, often leading to a fanatical zeal for what was "Chicano." Mexican American nationalism became a "natural response to 120 years of political, economic, and cultural suppression."[6] This Chicano nationalism focused on extolling the virtues of being a Mexican in the United States who had survived discrimination and marginalization and fought back politically or otherwise.

Mario Barrera similarly argues that the Chicano Movement "drew on the heritage of Chicano political activism" but "added distinctive new elements, such as the heavy involvement of youth and the emphasis on academic programs."[7] Barrera posits that Chicano youth perceived a political vacuum in traditional community politics as represented by Mexican American political groups and other middle-class organizations. These organizations were still preaching the moderate liberal agenda while African Americans were taking to the streets and white youths were closing down universities. The United States was in turmoil and many segments of the nation were questioning the legitimacy of traditional politics while these Mexican American groups still clung to their integrationist views. The students, says Barrera, became "hypersensitive" to the conditions of the *barrio* and saw themselves as the only ones bold enough to agitate for change. In a sense, the more Americanized students were confronting a cultural and generational gap that made them see their elders as being too passive at a time of heightened activism. Barrera argues that external conditions served as the principal catalysts for the Movement. The Kennedy election, the civil-rights movement, Lyndon Johnson's War on Poverty, the war in Vietnam, and the Free Speech Movement in Berkeley were all "stimulants" to Chicano student activism. Once stimulated, the community activists developed an ideological agenda that combined "communitarian and egalitarian goals . . . and what might be seen as an almost nostalgic vision of community." This vision, according to Barrera, never reached a refined phase, resulting in contradictions within the Movement.[8]

Juan Gómez-Quiñones defines the Chicano Movement as the liberal phase of Chicano political history. The twelve years between 1966 and 1978 were a "juncture between self-determination or integration."[9] Chicano reformers were disillusioned with the uneven progress in the areas of civil rights and economic betterment. The black civil-rights movement and the white antiwar movement made the liberal agenda seem even more inadequate as Chicanos saw dissatisfaction within those groups they perceived as having more influence on mainstream society. The Cuban Revolution and the African wars for independence, as well as the Mexican student movement, also galvanized "consciousness" among Chicanos. This consciousness was later given direction by the "Farm Workers Union, the Alianza, the Crusade for Justice, student organizations, and . . . La Raza Unida."[10] The Movement came to concentrate on the "questions of alienation, ethnicity, identity, class, gender, and chauvinism." The Movement, according to Gómez-Quiñones, became a struggle for self-identification and the search for a historical past.[11]

For Gómez-Quiñones, the academy, or at least Chicanos within it, contributed heavily to the search for identity and historical perspective. He argues that students were responsible for the development of the ideology of *chicanismo*. This ideology "emerged as a challenge to the dominant institutions, assumptions, politics, principles, political leaders, and organizations within and without the community." The emphasis on "dignity, self-worth, pride, uniqueness, feeling of cultural rebirth, and equal economic opportunity" became attractive to Mexican Americans across class, regional, and generational lines, since most had faced some form of discrimination in their lives.[12] From this *chicanismo* came the preoccupation with participation in community affairs, the securing of democratic rights and justice for the community, a commitment to developing parallel institutions and to opening existing ones to Mexican Americans, and a global solidarity with oppressed groups. The student-power movement provided a sense of homogeneity to a diverse community because its members identified themselves as Chicanos rather than *tejanos, californios,* or New Mexicans and because they identified themselves with national leaders and national issues. Paramount in this ideological hodgepodge was the search for an identity.[13]

Carlos Muñoz, the first major figure in the Movement to write about it in an autobiographical style, agrees on the question of identity. Muñoz describes the Movement as a social phenomenon placed in the "context of the politics of identity." For him, as with Gómez-Quiñones, students were the backbone of the drive for social change among Chicanos. Unlike Acuña, Muñoz does not see the Movement as simply another phase of the Chicano struggle for liberation. In fact, the Chicano student movement signaled a departure from the struggles of the past because of its youthful nature, its ideological tendencies, and its search for identity.[14] Working-class youths, many already at the universities, saw two major challenges confronting them. One was the atrocious conditions in the barrios, and the other was their isolation from the historical and cultural process. These were young people who decided to embark on a journey to recapture their culture, their history, and, primarily, their identity as Chicanos.[15] Like Barrera, Muñoz sees external factors as being important in the politicalization of this generation of young people. These students were moved by events taking place around them. They confronted an unjust war in which Chicanos were dying at a high rate; they were seeing the liberal Johnson years giving way to the Nixon administration; and they were constantly being reminded of white middle-class discontent and black anger. Most important, they were beginning to see their elders radicalizing their politics.[16]

Although the aforementioned scholars provided an intellectual foundation for studying the Chicano Movement, their works offer no synthesis of the steps the community took to make changes in its status. Without the synthesis, the Movement appears to be an emotional odyssey without defined objectives, and one more instance of Mexicans being riled. That, however, was not the case. The Chicano Movement was not simply a search for identity, or an outburst of collective anxiety. Rather, it was a full-fledged transformation of the way Mexican Americans thought, played politics, and promoted their culture. Chicanos embarked on a struggle to make fundamental changes, because only fundamental changes could make them active participants in their lives.

In this work, I discuss and analyze the steps taken by significant groups within the Mexican American community to develop a political consciousness, or ethos, that defined them as a distinct sector in American society. More focused than just a communal philosophy, a political ethos is the manner in which a community rationalizes and justifies its political participation in society. The development of that ethos requires that intellectuals, politicians, activists, and other influential individuals within a community assess their historical importance, recognize or decide on their class status or statuses, promote their cultural roots, and organize a political agenda. This process is neither uniform nor ideologically consistent throughout all sectors that embark on this philosophical odyssey. In fact, its diversity and often-contradictory nature maintain this activity as an ethos rather than a political ideology. But there is enough commonality and political unity to thrust the community toward a defined goal.

During the Movement, activists chose to identify certain symbols, events, rhetoric, and forms of resistance as being part of a pool of consciousness that gave meaning to the term Chicano, which came to denote those who fought for the rights of Mexican Americans and fought against Anglo-American racism. The Movement was driven by profound political and cultural ideas on being Chicano.[17] This activist philosophy came to be known as *chicanismo*. By popularizing these elements through rhetoric and debate, Chicano activists developed a cultural–political taxonomy that explained their activism. This taxonomy differed from those of the past, which were either pro-America or pro-Mexico. This new political identification was pro-barrio and incorporated Americanism with the barrio's Mexicanism. The negative aspects of the American experience combined with the historical nostalgia of Mexico to create a cultural milieu conducive to being Chicano. A large part of that ethos remains intact among Mexican American politicians, academicians, intellectuals, artists, and social workers today. Much of this ethos is now internalized and appears publicly only in times of major debate on ethnic issues or when Chicanos discuss things among themselves. But it continues to provide the premise for the activism of the present. None of the works previously cited succeed in explaining this militant ethos. Consequently, their analyses stop short and relegate the Movement to a particular time and place in history, with little regard for its legacy. According to them, once the shouting and marching stop, the Movement ends. The legacy is then measured only by the "changed" lives of the participants. If we ignore the ethos, the historical value of the Movement diminishes. And the Mexican American community reverts back to being an oppressed community that periodically rebels when it sees others do so or when conditions become unbearable. Once others stop rebelling, or conditions improve slightly, Mexican Americans go back to being the invisible minority. This, however, is contrary to what happened. Mexican Americans have not ceased to struggle, and they continue to develop indigenous leadership and to see themselves as part of a vibrant community with a proud heritage. Rather than become invisible, they have become a mainstay in the political and cultural arena in a large part of the United States. To this day, no synthesis has been provided for looking at the development of a militant ethos in the Mexican American community.

Reflection on this led me to attempt a synthesis of the historical data to explain the ethos that guided the Movement. In my quest to provide that synthesis, I identified four phases in the Movement. These phases contribute to a clearer picture of what occurred among the barrio's elite, the working class, and La Raza's artists and culturalists. (La Raza is a term used within the Mexican American community to refer to people of Latino descent.) In my analysis, the Movement was as much a series of phases as it was a series of events. In synthesizing the process of the Movement, I believe I offer a way to study the Movement that goes beyond anything that has been done before. It also allows the reader and scholar to understand the future implications of that Movement because each phase has its particular legacy.

In the first phase of the Movement, Mexican American intellectuals, politicians, students, and others came to believe that the liberal agenda, which had been seen as the solution to the community's problems, was simply morally corrupt and a failure. By liberal agenda I mean the traditional manner by which immigrants and minorities were supposed to integrate into the American mainstream. This would include education, good citizenship, patriotism, alliances with liberal groups, faith in government, and cultural assimilation. For Chicanos it also meant waiting for the problems of

African Americans to be solved. Mexican Americans of the pre-Movement period believed in a capitalist society without rigid class distinctions, where individual success was dependent on abilities or shortcomings. Solutions were within their grasp and progress assured for all who truly sought it. Added to that was often a faith in American institutions, a strong anti-Communist or antiforeign bias, and a disdain for militant ethnic or group consciousness. Although they engaged in numerous reform campaigns, Mexican Americans of the pre-Movement period continued to believe in the fundamental goodness and "fairness" of American society.

Time and time again, Mexican Americans had attempted to reach out to the mainstream by developing patriotic organizations, serving in the armed forces in large numbers, adopting American ideals, and de-emphasizing their national origins. Yet they remained outside the mainstream and saw the gap widening between them and other Americans. The liberal agenda de-Mexicanized them but failed to Americanize them as a group, allowing them into the mainstream as individuals, not as a community. Even this entrance had limited benefits, since Americans of Mexican descent continued to be targets of racism and cultural insensitivity. Mexican Americans were allowed into the American mainstream to the degree that they rejected their "Mexicanness" or diluted their historical experience. A false historical experience became the "Spanish" missions, the *fiestas,* the Mexican participants in the Alamo, and the "Frito Bandito."

Chicano activists lost faith in an abundant society, rejected the notion of a classless America, and questioned the historical continuity with American society that some of its elders argued existed. This continuity was best understood through the study of the Mexican "contribution" to American society and the philosophical similarities between Mexican Americans and Anglo-Americans. Chicano intellectuals rejected this kind of historical interpretation. They no longer saw the value of patriotism or of liberal leaders. In their eyes, American institutions, such as the government, schools, churches, and social agencies, had failed. American institutions, as far as activists were concerned, were inherently racist. In the passion of the Movement, many activists even lost faith in a pluralistic society, arguing that pluralism often meant diluting their cultural and philosophical ideas in order to belong to the whole, which remained dominated by those who believed in capitalism, regarded African Americans as the only oppressed minority, and had no historical understanding of the Mexican American experience.

The rejection of the liberal agenda led to a search for new solutions— solutions that were oriented inward, born of experience, and based on cultural and philosophical tendencies native to the community. New leaders arose who were part of the community, and the organizations they founded shunned assimilation and sought legitimacy not from the integrationist middle class but from the nationalistic working class. These organizations accentuated their ethnic culture for organizing purposes and tended to be wary of liberal condescension. In rejecting the liberal agenda, Chicano activists sought to destroy the sense of inadequacy that many Mexican Americans felt in their relationship with mainstream society. It thus emboldened many to fill the vacuum of leadership that developed when Anglo-Americans and middle-class Mexican Americans lost legitimacy in the numerous barrios across the country. Numerous organizations, such as the Crusade for Justice in Colorado, La Raza Unida Party in Texas, and the Alianza Federal de Pueblos Libres in New Mexico, competed with the League of United Latin American Citizens, the American G.I. Forum, the Political Association of Spanish-Speaking Organizations, and other integrationist organizations to be the activist entities of the Mexican American community. Other organizations, such as the Mexican American Legal Defense and Education Fund, the Southwest Voter Registration and Education Drive and the Mexican American Democrats, which staked out a ground between the two extremes, also arose during this time.

In the second phase, Mexican American activists saw a need to reinterpret the past. They knew that Mexican Americans could overcome their powerlessness only if they could see themselves as a historical people with heroes, legends, triumphs, and legacies. Chicano historians discovered old heroes and reinterpreted old events through a new nationalist framework that made Mexican Americans active participants in history. This reinterpretation led Mexican Americans to discard the stereotypes of the lazy, passive, *mañana*-oriented *mexicano* and replace it with the proud, historically rich Chicano or Chicana, who was ready to fight for his or her community. Scholars, writers, dramatists, poets, and essayists found new protagonists in the forgotten history. They discovered revolutionists, journalists, lawyers, union organizers, and others who had fought against an overwhelming

Anglo-American onslaught. Also, reinterpretation allowed Mexican Americans to shift the blame for many of the barrio's problems from themselves to American society. They now saw poverty, alienation, and political powerlessness as a result of the U.S. conquest of the Southwest and subsequent colonization, segregation, and racism. History, once used to perpetuate stereotypes and rationalize Mexican American backwardness, became a weapon for liberation. It also allowed for a growth of an academic as well as an organic or homegrown Chicano intellectual elite that sought to give meaning to the Mexican American experience.

The third phase led Chicano activists, intellectuals, and artists to affirm a rediscovered pride in their racial and class status and in their sense of peoplehood.[18] They emphasized their indigenous past and glorified the ancient civilizations of Mexico and South America. This connection to racial origins gave Mexican Americans historicity. It became okay to be brown. *Prietos* (those with brown complexions) were beautiful too! By accentuating their class status, Chicano activists and their adherents were able to legitimize, and at times romanticize, the lives of those who lived in the barrio. Mexican Americans, particularly the youth, did not have to be embarrassed by the music they heard, the food they ate, the *curanderas* who cured their illnesses, or the homegrown philosophies shared across countless kitchen tables. This affirmation of race and class brought about a sense of solidarity with Third World movements for liberation and united Chicanos with a worldwide revolution against oppression. It also spurred a renaissance of Chicano literature, theater, and art. Artists and writers now took the barrio as the setting for their work, and the working people or their indigenous ancestors as the protagonists. The attempt by earlier artists to integrate their works into the mainstream ceased among many of the new and some of the old artists of the barrio. The search began for a "uniquely Chicano" literature, theater, and art.

In the fourth phase, Chicano activists engaged in oppositional politics. They developed platforms, manifestos, and tactics that best represented an oppositional strategy to the American mainstream. Rather than simply make things bearable for Mexican Americans, Chicano activists sought to empower their community to free it from Anglo-American politicians, nativist educational curriculums, and cultural stereotypes. By engaging in oppositional politics, Chicano activists could emphasize the "Mexicanness" of the community and steer it away from integration into American society. To this end, they created their own political party, developed nationalist and quasi-socialist platforms, and manipulated local government agencies to be pro-Chicano and anti-Anglo. Chicano activists sought to question fundamentally the "goodness" of American society and undo the effects of years of segregation, discrimination, poverty, and political powerlessness. This I call the politics of Aztlán (the mythical birthplace of the Aztec nation; also the name Chicano activists gave to the land lost in the U.S.-Mexico war) because these political ideas were developed within a new framework that saw Mexican Americans as a historically and culturally rich community seeking to liberate itself from Anglo-American racism.[19] There were no more efforts to emulate traditional American politics. Grassroots politics that sought active participation by people in the barrio became the norm. Organizations of the barrio moved away from hierarchical structures, and in some areas well-educated activists became staff members of organizations rather than leaders to allow barrio residents to develop leadership skills.

Charismatic leaders, however, did arise, as they do in all movements. The barrio residents simply lacked too many leadership skills for them to assume the lead. Consequently, a group of men and some women became dominant in the Movement and would eventually come into conflict with each other. Their regional experiences led them to clash when they practiced politics at the national level. Still, these Movement leaders, more than the ones from the various moderate organizations, created for the Mexican American community a sense of national presence. That is, because they shared a political commonality and reinterpreted history in the same manner, they provided Chicanos with a sense of homogeneity. This *caudillismo* or leadership by personality would, however, eventually clash with the participatory approach of the barrios' politics.

In describing the four phases, I do not reconstruct the day-to-day activities of the Movement participants, nor do I discuss the cultural infrastructure of the Mexican American community. In this manner I differ from others who have written about political ideology in the Chicano community. The Movement never developed a centralized leadership. There were too many Chicano activist organizations with regional agendas and entrenched leaders. Although there were attempts to build a national umbrella, those efforts ended in vain. I shy away from an in-depth discussion of the Mexican

American community of the 1960s and 1970s and instead deal with ideas that found fertile ground at the national level, even though many were practiced at the local and regional level. In fact, although the activities of the Movement developed regionally, the Movement ethos quickly became national and then moved downward. This happened because a number of Chicano activists developed a wide following quite quickly, and their rhetoric became disseminated to regional groups through Movimiento newspapers and traveling activists. What brought these communities together initially were ideas that "intellectually" transcended regional differences.

My interest is to tie together the organizations and individuals that proved to be the principal players during this activist period. The Movimiento groups I focus on most are the United Farm Workers Union, the Crusade for Justice, the Alianza Federal de Pueblos Libres, and La Raza Unida Party. These were the largest, most active, and most prominent organizations during the Movement, and they were involved in every major event of the time period. From them came the most recognizable leaders. Some scholars argue that César Chávez's farmworkers' union and the Alianza were not part of the Movement because they never emphasized their *chicanismo*. I counter by saying that these two organizations were fundamental to the development of the militancy of the period. They contributed symbolism, rhetoric, and political and cultural confrontations with the mainstream that added to the militancy and nationalism of the times. And the historical record shows that most activists and participants considered the two as part of the Movement.

The four phases, although at times sequentially inconsistent, provided an aperture for different sectors within the Mexican American community to enter the philosophical discourse on being Chicano. Intellectuals debated, politicians campaigned, artists drew, *corridistas* sang, and writers wrote. For women, the Movement provided an opportunity for them to regain their historical role as strugglers on behalf of the barrio and the *familia*. Even as Chicanos attempted to develop a cultural nationalist philosophy, Chicanas challenged traditional Mexican orthodoxy. Rejection of the liberal agenda meant that new ground rules had to be established. The fact that women were among the first members of nearly every Chicano organization of the period meant that the Chicano Movement would be the most inclusive of all the social movements of the 1960s and 1970s, allowing—at times only grudgingly—women to serve at most levels except the very top.

The reinterpretation of history provided Chicanas an opportunity to discover their historical importance: as Aztec goddesses, as union organizers, as radical journalists, and as *soldaderas*. In a history of struggle against oppression, Chicanas fought against the greatest odds and remained faithful to the end. The cultural renaissance that made the third phase possible depended heavily on women. As transmitters and nurturers of the culture, the status of Chicanas grew in the eyes of the nationalist men and, more importantly, in their own eyes. Whether feminist or family-oriented, Chicana activists heavily promoted the image of women in struggle. In reality, Chicanos could be different only if the women were different. Although most Movimiento men remained limited in their feminism, most Chicanas transcended the limitations of cultural nationalism. In the politics of opposition, Chicanas were to play their biggest part. From the lettuce fields of southern California and the urban jungles of Colorado to the political offices of La Raza Unida Party in Texas, Chicanas remained a political presence throughout the Movimiento period. So strong was their presence that they split into Movement feminists and Movement loyalists.

The four-phase view of the Movement offers a new synthesis by which to study this activist period in the life of the Mexican American community. As compared with a narrative or even a class-based analysis, this synthesis best captures the interclass, intergenerational, and intergender coalescing that took place to form the militant ethos. This ethos, I argue, is irreversible. Although some of the militancy has been lost, and nationalism is subsumed by practical politics, the militant ethos remains even during the current period of Hispanic politics. Mexican American politicians still reject the old traditional liberal approach to civil rights and upward mobility, which disdained race-specific strategies and demanded assimilation. They see history in much the same way Chicano activist historians taught it,[20] and they have become ethnic politicians, accentuating the racial and cultural differences with the mainstream. Finally, they still practice a politics of opposition, though they do this within the context of coalition politics. That is, they continue to identify issues and carry out strategies uniquely appropriate for their communities and then find alliances that allow them to promote these issues. Hispanics, although often less than militant in their pursuit of change, no longer see themselves as just Americans. Rather, they are an ethnic group that has a historical notion of itself and whose importance lies within its uniqueness. In this sense, like the Mexican American Generation of the 1930s to 1960s, and the Chicano Movement Generation of the 1960s and 1970s, it has its own ethos and generational thought.

By using the four-phase framework in studying the Movement, we can recognize it as more than a passing phase in Mexican American history. We then understand it as a critical period in bringing the Mexican American community into the latter part of the twentieth century. It better identifies the changes that took place within the Mexican American community than the previous narratives or analyses. This framework captures the grass-roots, democratic tendencies of the Movement by showing how a new dialogue occurs that includes voices from a number of sectors within the community that had never participated before. This approach also does not relegate the Movement to the political graveyard as an unfocused, passionate social catharsis that arose, played itself out, and left things worse than they were before. This is the kind of conclusion that comes from some previous studies, which start out praising the ideals of the Movement, then criticize its ideological foundations and bemoan its stepchild, the Hispanic Generation. We can, through this synthesis, see the Movement as a process by which the Mexican American community comes to debate its place in American history and society. Mexican Americans no longer react to problems confronting them as would immigrants, or as an ethnic group that is slowly fading into assimilation. Rather, Mexican Americans confront the challenges of a still-race-conscious society through ethnic-group solidarity and through strategies that guarantee their survival as a distinct yet very American community.

Methodologically, I have devoted one chapter of the book to each phase of the Movement, one to the testing of the process in Robstown, Texas, and a concluding chapter to summarizing the process. In this last chapter, I provide a cursory analysis of the Hispanic Generation and the politics of that generation. What is evident in this methodology is that the phases are not sequential in regard to observable time periods. That is, it is not the case that phase one takes two years, followed by phase two, and so on. Rather, the process is sequential in that each phase can only be fully developed if the previous phase has occurred or has begun occurring. It is then reasonable that each phase will contain elements of the other three. In presenting the different phases in their separate chapters, I will discuss rhetoric and strategies that are relevant to all the phases.

In addition to using primary sources to understand this period, the organizations, and the ideas that formed the Chicano Movement, I have also interpreted a large number of secondary works. I do this to show how a number of books, articles, essays, and written ideas were influential in the development of strategies, platforms, manifestos, and ideologies. By this approach I do not attempt to reconstruct day-to-day events; rather, I seek to highlight ideas and rhetoric. The ideas and the rhetoric I discuss are those that found fertile ground in the minds and hearts of Chicanos and were repeated continually, in most cases finding their way into publication. A discussion of these works' influence in developing a Chicano militant ethos is thus important, notwithstanding the fact that they fall into the category of secondary sources.

I also decided to use a partial-ethnographic approach. By this I mean that in certain parts of the book I refer to experiences and empirical data gained through personal participation in the Movement. This, I felt, would best place this work in its proper perspective. To imply that I am an unbiased scholar is at best unethical. I participated in the Movement, edited a community underground newspaper, served as chairman of La Raza Unida Party in Kleberg County, Texas, and cochaired the last statewide political campaign for the party in Texas. For a period of four years, I was immersed in political activism and looked at the world through Chicano-colored glasses. Like many other activists, I sacrificed studies and a career to make Aztlán a reality. That experience and the emotions generated from it will always temper what I write. I accept that I have biases that seep through my writing.

I believe, however, that this does not diminish the importance of this work. On the contrary, the strength of this partial ethnography lies in the fact that, as a participant who was recruited to the Movement, participated without restraint, and then left with mixed feelings, I have a desire to see the complexities of that Movement deciphered. What attracted many young men and women to this movement for social reform? What made many of us deviate from what would have been relatively successful lives? After all, we were the lucky few who were in college, and we knew the system well enough to survive and possibly prosper in it. Why, unlike Mexican Americans during the integrationist years of the 1940s and 1950s, did Chicanos seek a different course? No longer satisfied with pluralism and liberal agendas, Chicanos and Chicanas rejected mainstream American society and clung to the idea of Aztlán—a social, political, economic, and cultural utopia, free of liberal politicians, welfare programs, police brutality, discrimination, poverty, and identity crises.

This work does not follow a strict chronological time frame. It does, nevertheless, provide a historical perspective. Because the end product is an assessment of a constructed ethos, I mesh together ideas and events that occurred years apart. Their importance is not when they developed but that they developed at all. This approach allows the versatility that a traditional history could not to tell the history of a Movement that represented the yearnings of a people long neglected and disdained by a society that only a few years before had seemed so admirable to many of them.

CHAPTER ONE

Rejecting the Liberal Agenda

When the League of United Latin American Citizens (LULAC) was launched in 1929, most of its participants believed that citizenship and education would solve many, if not most, of the Mexican American community's problems. The organization's participants were not so much naive as they were hopeful that if Mexican Americans cast their lot with American society, their own would improve. Going back to Mexico, as some had done before, no longer remained an option by the 1920s. Mexican intellectual thought had also ceased to be a factor in the philosophy of a small but growing Mexican American middle class, which had been born in the United States and educated in an American school system devoid of diversity. The LULAC Code succinctly described the view of these individuals, mostly men: "Respect your citizenship, conserve it, honor your country, maintain its traditions in the minds of your children, incorporate yourself in the culture and civilization."[1]

The founders of LULAC did not seek to renounce their origins. Instead, they sought to "maintain a sincere and respectful reverence for [our] racial origin."[2] However, they believed that "Americanization" was important in order for Mexican Americans to gain their full rights. It seemed obvious to leaders such as Alonso Perales and M. C. González that state and local authorities recognized only those who were citizens and knew their voting rights.[3] If Mexican Americans were going to make changes in their status, they had to do it within the established process. The more militant unionism of the early 1900s and the leftist politics of the Partido Liberal Mexicano had led to an increase in nativism and discrimination. The Mexicanist philosophies of the earlier activists had often been Mexico-oriented and did not encourage integration into American society. This activism also tended to be working class based and thus seemingly exclusive of middle-class integrationist strains. Middle-class reformers saw integration as a better option for being treated with respect.[4] These new middle-class men—and the few women who shared their views—sought a philosophy that provided answers to questions about their status in American society. By the late 1930s, this small but growing generation had identified itself as American first. World War II only further clarified this generation's identity, as many Mexican Americans enlisted and fought against fascism and tyranny. In the process, the men became the country's most decorated ethnic group, and the women distinguished themselves in home-front victory committees and in defense-industry jobs.[5] From the great conflict came a group of men and women ready to claim what they assumed their valor entitled them to have.[6] They sought access to the nation's institutions and an integration that allowed them to benefit from the prosperity of the postwar era. Their war experience had increased their own certainty that they were Americans and should be seen as such by others. Still, most of them sought to attain this prosperity and upward mobility without giving up their culture completely. They were Americans, but they would not stop being Mexican. They lived in or near the barrio, and their professional or business endeavors depended on the Mexican American community, a large part of which was less integrated into American society than they. Many also felt an obligation to stay close to their community. They preferred the dual role of American and Mexican.

By the mid-1950s, much of Mexican America had shifted away from this dualism as the anti-Communist sentiment had grown in strength. To offset the potential red-baiting, LULAC and other middle-class organizations emphasized their Americanism over their cultural roots. But they did so while remaining confident of their *mexicanismo*. In the 1940s and the beginning of the 1950s, Americanization posed no threat to the self-identity of many of the Mexican American leaders. For these leaders, Americanization was a way to develop a group identity that would empower them in the struggle for their rights as citizens. But the constant promotion of Americanization, the continual concern with legitimacy, and the overall better economic conditions many of them attained cemented them emotionally and philosophically to mainstream society and away from their Mexicanness.

Another force in the Americanization process was the widespread repatriation and deportation campaigns that occurred periodically from the Depression through the 1950s. These campaigns decimated some of the more traditional Mexican communities, some of which never regained their former stability as Mexican entities. Mexican Americans recognized their tenuous position in American society as they saw their neighbors, both those with legal and those with illegal status, become victims of American nativism. Many of them saw the need to move toward Americanization. This forced removal by deportation divided the Mexican American community into legal and illegal, adding a judicial distinction to the class distinctions already present in the community. Those who were illegal, or who were oriented culturally and politically toward Mexico, became the less dominant intellectual or social force in the community, whereas those who chose Americanization became the new power brokers in the barrio.[7]

These new Mexican Americans and their sympathizers fought almost unceasingly to change conditions in the barrio, particularly those in the schools. Having faith in the American system, and being quite aware of their status as an electorally weak constituency, they challenged their second-class status through the courts. They were successful in cases such as *Mendez v. Westminster School District* (1946), which struck down segregation based on race; *Delgado v. Bastrop Independent School District* (1948), which made school officials accountable for maintaining an unsegregated environment; and the Pete Hernandez criminal case (1954), in which Gus García, Carlos Cadena, and John J. Herrera argued that Mexican Americans were protected by the Fourteenth Amendment in the selection of juries.[8] Their success in calling attention to their cause accelerated their desires to participate actively in politics. They established organizations that supported liberal candidates for office at the national and local levels. In 1957, Mexican Americans elected Raymond L. Telles mayor of El Paso, and in 1961, Henry B. González was elected to Congress in Texas, followed by Edward Roybal in 1962 in California. In 1960, many Mexican Americans had joined the Kennedy campaign, forming Viva Kennedy clubs throughout the Southwest, which was the most significant venture by Mexican Americans into the national political arena up to that time.[9]

Shortly before and then after the war, there were also several leftist organizations that fought for the rights of the Mexican American population.

These organizations, while dedicated to the advancement of the Mexican American, were tied to the national reform movements greatly influenced by the American Communist Party. Theirs was a popular-front approach to liberal politics. Like similar leftist organizations of their time, the Asociación Nacional Mexico-Americana (1949–54), the Spanish-Speaking Congress (1939–49), and others understood the working-class nature of the Mexican American community.[10] Most Mexican Americans were unskilled workers, and much of their oppression was economic. But they were not blind to the attacks that Mexican Americans suffered because of their national origin. They understood that discrimination added to the difficulties of poor Mexican Americans. They were conscious, however, that educated, well-integrated Mexican Americans suffered discrimination too.

Despite the intensity of their struggle, and their empathy toward cultural nationalism, these organizations took an integrative approach to their politics.[11] They were radical reformers involved in what Mario García calls "democratic reformism" on behalf of their community. They found much that was good in the New Deal and the progressive campaigns of Henry Wallace and other left-of-center groups. These reformers believed that the Declaration of Independence and the Constitution provided the framework under which Mexican Americans could become first-class citizens.[12] They sought to work with existing groups and to use the court system to destroy the obstacles that impeded their economic and political mobility. These were native-born middle- and lower-middle-class Mexican Americans whose definition of Americanism included cultural and political pluralism of the democratic kind.

By the beginning of the 1960s, however, most of the truly militant organizations had been decimated by McCarthyism and the Cold War. LULAC and the American G.I. Forum were still operating but had by then become more concerned with scholarships, Mexican fiestas, self-help campaigns, desegregation, and poll-tax drives. These two organizations had come to accept the reality that integration would take longer than anticipated and that programs based on race or national origin were an acceptable part of the equalization process that would lead to full integration.[13] This was a concept they had rejected before as being segregationist in nature.

The passing of the civil-rights mantle from the Mexican American Generation to the Chicano Generation may best be understood by looking at

Mexican American political activity from 1960 to 1964. In the late summer of 1960, a number of American G.I. Forum leaders founded the Viva Kennedy clubs to support the presidential candidacy of John F. Kennedy. Between August and November, these Mexican American activists established several hundred clubs throughout the Southwest and as far north as Pennsylvania, Indiana, Ohio, and Illinois. They were joined by Puerto Ricans in New York and Cubans in Florida in support of the Democratic candidate. The Viva Kennedy effort sought to call attention to the potential of Mexican American voters in a tight election. It was also a way to wring some federal appointments from a future Kennedy administration.[14] The Viva Kennedy campaign took off in a way that surprised even the most optimistic Mexican American politicians. Many volunteers came forward, especially from the Mexican American middle class, which found itself anxious to share its skills and to make a name for itself. Democratic voter rolls were greatly enhanced by new Mexican American voters throughout the Southwest and other places where large numbers of Latino voters resided. On election day, Mexican Americans and other Latinos came out in record numbers.[15] In Texas, they gave Kennedy a 200,000-vote plurality to overcome the Anglo-American voters' split that favored Richard M. Nixon. In New Mexico, Mexican American voters helped Kennedy win the state by 7,000 votes. They also helped him win in Illinois, and in California, they came close to putting him over the top.[16]

Mexican American leaders such as Dennis Chávez of New Mexico, Edward Roybal of California, and Hector P. García of Texas expected Kennedy to respond to this support with appointments to his administration and to the federal bench. Robert Kennedy had implied that numerous appointments in the foreign service might be available, but no promises had been made. Being naive politicians, Viva Kennedy leaders had left it to the goodwill of the new president. They would quickly learn a lesson in broker politics, as other groups that had bargained gained appointments and Mexican Americans were mostly left out.[17] Even some of the appointments received by Mexican Americans turned out to be others than those suggested by club leaders.[18] Shortly after the election, when the reality of their powerlessness became clear, the Viva Kennedy club leaders moved to organize a national political structure. They formed the Political Association of the Spanish-Speaking Organizations (PASSO) in 1961. Members of PASSO were a slightly different breed from those of earlier groups like LULAC and the American G.I. Forum. These were men and women who saw the need to take one step further in their political development. The organization was led by fiery leaders who articulated a new militancy. These leaders were more aggressive in their demands for equality and were willing to take on mainstream institutions in a political fight. They demanded action on the part of government. Much like the black civil-rights leaders of the time, they divided Anglo-America into a dual society—one compassionate and progressive, the other racist and conservative. When they attacked the latter, they did not feel unpatriotic. These leaders had ties to labor and to war veterans, and their sense of community led them to seek to include all. By the 1960s, they felt that an atmosphere of change was coming to the barrios of the Southwest. The Kennedy and Johnson rhetoric, the social programs, and a small but rising militant middle class made up of social workers, bureaucrats, and labor organizers provided an image of a groundswell. Yet, at the height of this perceived groundswell, the direction of the Mexican American community's struggle for civil rights changed, and so did much of its leadership. Initially, PASSO leaders attempted to build a national organization, but before the end of the year, only Texas and a few northern communities had chapters. The organization endorsed politicians and encouraged Mexican Americans to run for elected office.[19] Unfortunately, the majority of those they endorsed in the Texas statewide elections in 1962 were defeated. Again, they showed their political immaturity by endorsing candidates who they thought could win but who were not popular with Mexican American voters. Badly beaten, they changed strategies in 1963 by selecting a slate of Mexican Americans to run for the city council in Crystal City, Texas.[20]

Known as the "first revolt," this election epitomized the attitudes and ideals of much of that generation's reformers. It became a point of departure for the Movement. In 1963, PASSO leaders united with the International Brotherhood of Teamsters to organize an electoral challenge to the Anglo-controlled city government of the predominantly Mexican American community of Crystal City in an area known as the Winter Garden. This challenge had arisen from a desire to make the town friendly toward unionization and to test a new approach in Mexican American civil-rights efforts. A slate of five semi-illiterate Mexican Americans swept the city council elections. The victory sent shock waves throughout the state. Albert Peña, the president of PASSO, and Albert Fuentes, the executive secretary, both of whom directed the challenge from San Antonio, vowed to use the same strategy that had elected "Los Cinco" (The Five) throughout the state. Many Mexican American activists and their liberal supporters applauded the victory and saw the emergence of a new militant attitude.[21] It was an attitude, however, much within the mainstream of liberal electoral politics. Unfortunately for Peña and Fuentes, not all Mexican American leaders saw the victory as positive, nor as the appropriate way in which Mexican Americans could integrate into the political and social mainstream. They saw the action of Los Cinco as an attempt at separatism, or at least discrimination in reverse. The PASSO strategy, they argued, went against the more legitimate and dignified approach of court litigation. Also, Hector P. García, the national president of PASSO, questioned the ties to the Teamsters union. García, as well as others, were proponents of going it alone. They believed that only Mexican Americans could speak for Mexican Americans, at least at the local level. Although often the more militant sounding, Peña and Fuentes tended to believe in liberal coalitions. At the PASSO convention the following year, the opponents of the Crystal City revolt, led by García, made the election a major issue of contention. This led to a split that eventually doomed the organization.[22]

The failure to unite behind Los Cinco of Crystal City revealed an Achilles' heel in the liberal agenda of these Mexican American leaders. Mexican American reformers found themselves too immature politically to unite behind one strategy. Some, radicalized by the inability to make significant changes in the social structure of Texas despite numerous legal challenges, saw the Crystal City event as a new approach, a way to finally crack the Anglo-American dominance in areas where Mexican Americans were the majority. Others felt they had to walk a fine line between activism and citizenship. Rather than see Los Cinco's victory as the wave of the future, a way in which Mexican Americans could take control of their own political fortunes, these reformers considered the working-class revolution an embarrassment manipulated by outsiders who had not chosen the candidates well. To many of them it represented an aberration from the many legitimate and dignified judicial campaigns they had waged. The five Crystal City candidates had nothing in common with the lawyers, educators, or professional types. That they were inefficient, fought among themselves, and were even caught violating the law horrified many middle-class Mexican Americans who equated integration with immaculate citizenship.[23] They condemned Los Cinco for discriminating in reverse and sought to move away from that kind of militancy. PASSO would engage in a number of other local elections, but these were no longer promoted publicly as "revolts" because of the Anglo-American backlash and the split in the membership. PASSO would continue to function until the late sixties, but its influence had badly declined by the end of 1964.

Despite the few political victories and the successful legal challenges, it became difficult for many to see significant changes in the barrios. What economic changes had occurred seemed more to be individual phenomena that "coincided with a general upward coasting with the national economy."[24] Those whose lives had improved significantly could see that they were the "only(ies)" in their community, individuals who had made it despite the obstacles.[25] As the civil-rights movement began to spread throughout the South, Mexican Americans saw that some of their communities were no better off than the dilapidated ghettos being shown on national television. The migrant communities of South Texas and southern California and the rural *rancherías* of New Mexico were only slightly less poverty stricken than those rural Mississippi and Louisiana towns that most of the national television audience saw. The only difference between the desperation of the unemployed in the urban ghettos of the north and that which Mexican Americans experienced in Denver, East Los Angeles, San Antonio, and El Paso was the size of the population involved.

With regard to the school systems, Mexican Americans could argue that their schools were just as segregated and inadequate as any found in the South or North. In 1960, only 13 percent of all Mexican Americans had a high school education and less than 6 percent had attended college.[26] The dropout rate for many school districts with large numbers of Mexican Americans remained high. Those who stayed in school faced inadequate educational systems that often tracked them into remedial or "slow" classes and away from college preparatory courses. Vocational shops and Reserve Officer Training Corps were the mainstay of many of these schools. Rampant discrimination was also a constant. In schools where they were a minority, Mexican American students were seen as an educational burden, potential troublemakers, and students who needed little attention since they were likely to drop out. In schools where they were the majority, they still found themselves with inadequate facilities, poor curriculums, and underrepresentation among student leaders, cheerleaders, and homecoming queens. Quotas that limited the number of Mexican American student leaders or athletes existed, if not de jure at least de facto.[27] This type of treatment often led to hostility and alienation and manifested itself in large numbers of gangs and individuals in trouble with the law.

The effects of an inadequate educational system were apparent in the economic condition of Mexican American families. Only 19 percent of Mexican American workers were employed in white-collar jobs. Over 50 percent worked in low-skill jobs that earned them only forty-seven cents for every dollar their white counterparts made. This rate of pay kept nearly four out of every ten Mexican Americans below the poverty level. Unemployment in the barrios of the Southwest was twice as high as that of white workers and only slightly less than that of black workers.[28] Many Mexican Americans, unable to find work, joined the army of migrants who traveled from state to state picking crops. Nearly 16 percent of the Mexican American population worked in the fields. Once there, few of them had the skills to leave the migrant stream, and most of them lived in areas where there were no jobs at all. If they were lucky, they worked for four to six months of the year in the fields and then performed odd jobs for the other six to eight months. The possibility that the cycle would be broken seemed remote, since most migrant children did not finish the school year because of the traveling.[29]

In 1940, George I. Sánchez's book *Forgotten People* described the situation of the Hispano of New Mexico in the following manner: "It should be quite clear that the problems faced by New Mexicans cannot be attacked piecemeal nor in terms of individual communities. The problems are regional ones and they do not observe county or state lines, or subdivisions of population. . . . For many of us things are better than they were once. But mine are still forgotten people."[30] Nearly twenty-five years later, the same could still be said of most Mexican Americans in the Southwest and throughout the United States. The growth of the population had exceeded the limited openings in a still-race-conscious society. The few victories in educational reform and civil rights had failed to keep up with the disadvantages that continued to multiply for a community with limited marketable skills and a high dropout rate.

By the early 1960s, many Mexican Americans were disenchanted with traditional liberal politics. These liberal politics centered on an active government that would provide economic development, protect civil rights, and guarantee cultural pluralism. It was an approach that required faith in the established institutions and patience in the face of slow change. It was a steady approach of government action, judicial litigation, and Anglo-American leadership. It also required that Mexican Americans wait for the "real" civil-rights problems—those of black Americans—to be solved before the focus shifted to them. Carlos Guerra, Chicano activist and writer, succinctly described the dilemma when he described Mexican Americans as "not white enough to be accepted and not black enough for the civil rights movement." Mexican American activists began to feel frustrated. Court litigation, the creation of patriotic organizations, and the support of liberal candidates seemed to have had a limited effect on the majority of Mexicans and Mexican Americans, who continued to struggle with poverty and discrimination.

If Mexican Americans had been able to see their efforts from a historical perspective, they would have realized how effective their struggles had been. They had successfully challenged most of the state and school board policies supporting segregation, they had won inclusion in the protective umbrella of the Fourteenth Amendment, they had forced schools to upgrade the educational facilities used by Mexican American students, they had won local and regional elections, and they had made it difficult for blatant racism to be expressed openly in the media. The perception of many of them of Mexican America, however, was clouded by the lingering poverty, the de facto segregated schools, the stereotypes that frequently appeared in the media, and the fear of being left out of the civil-rights movement. Mexican American middle-class leaders saw a need for an accelerated struggle, but their liberal politics simply did not provide a mechanism for this new reform effort. Their political ideology had been nurtured during the Cold War and their Americanism defined by their patriotism in time of war. To engage in un-American activities or to endorse radical ideas did not seem an alternative for the majority.[31] Yet discontent prevailed among Mexican American activists and leaders. Even the bastion of liberal-reform admiration, Hector P. García, at times slipped into despair. In 1961, in a letter to his friend Manuel Avila, Jr., a state department official serving in Venezuela, he wrote: "I don't think that we can expect anything from the Anglo politicians. . . . They want us to help them but they don't want to give us a break. What else can we do?"[32] And again several months later: "The Negroes seem to be doing alright, the Italian-American seems to be doing alright, the Polish-American seems to be doing alright, but why in the Lord's name we cannot organize our people . . . I do not know."[33]

Compounding the discontent was the diminishing influence of some of the Mexican American elected officials. By playing militant politics within the system, they became targets of conservative reaction. In San Antonio, Albert Peña's Mexican American–Liberal coalition suffered a major setback in the mid-1960s, which led to the loss of his county commissioner's seat.[34] In New Mexico, Manuel Lujan, a conservative Republican, replaced Dennis Chávez as the main Mexican American political force. And by 1961, El Paso had returned to Anglo-American control after Telles opted to become an ambassador. The death of John F. Kennedy deeply shook many Mexican Americans. Although Lyndon Baines Johnson followed with an array of social programs, he did not inspire the same enthusiasm among Mexican Americans as did Kennedy. Said Raul Morín, an official of the American G.I. Forum, "The tragic death of President Kennedy has left the whole picture of the Spanish-speaking in the Southwest jumbled."[35]

The limitation of these leaders' influence reflected the Mexican American community's reluctance to engage in mainstream electoral politics. The working class remained largely unaffected by liberal change, and the middle class remained divided. Some saw the need to continue agitation, but others became complacent or simply did not see how further activism could benefit them.[36] Any change in the intensity of the Mexican American struggle depended not on the middle class but on the participation of the poorer, less integrated working class. But this large sector of the population failed to be inspired by the traditional politics of the liberal agenda. This agenda, although providing legal recourse, had simply not removed the physical obstacles to economic mobility, political power, or social integration. Those Anglo-Americans who favored the "old ways" had found ways to circumvent the laws, and they acted with impunity in discriminating against Mexican

Americans. The preoccupation of liberals with the rights of black Americans left little time for the barrios of the Southwest and Midwest. Integrationist politics that promoted Americanism often demeaned Mexican cultural characteristics. These politics did not inspire loyalty among the working class. By the 1960s, Mexican Americans seemed anxious for another strategy that empowered them as Mexicans and not as potential "good citizens." An alternative to assimilative politics had to come.

One of the first Mexican American activists to understand this was César Chávez, who in 1965 headed the National Farm Workers Association (NFWA) in California. He had been an organizer for the Community Service Organization before he founded the union. A traditional liberal group, the Community Service Organization sought to empower people by getting them involved in community issues. Its leaders were trained in Saul Alinsky's school for radicals, but its methods were far from radical, since it concentrated on putting pressure on welfare organizations and city government to improve services to people in the community. When Chávez tried to steer the organization into organizing farmworkers and giving them bargaining power to improve their lives, its leadership resisted. That type of organizing went beyond the organization's agenda. Chávez soon realized that service organizations did not empower people, they simply placated them or minimized their frustration. They also did not build organic leadership but kept poor Mexican Americans dependent on professional social reformers. When he left the Community Service Organization, he did so to help farmworkers gain collective bargaining power. On September 16, 1965, Chávez called his first *huelga* (strike) against California growers.[37] Citing the *Grito de Dolores*, or "Cry of Dolores," which launched Mexico's independence movement, Chávez proclaimed a struggle to liberate the Mexican American farmworker. Although the NFWA was nonviolent and somewhat in the tradition of the American union movement, it helped launch the Chicano Movement. The sight of poor Mexican American farmworkers in the picket lines, carrying a banner of the *Virgen de Guadalupe,* struck a nationalist nerve in many Mexican Americans. The fact that these semiliterate workers were organizing meetings, writing propaganda, and negotiating union contracts cast a new and more empowering light on Mexican Americans. These farmworkers had taken it upon themselves to change their condition, and they were doing it despite harassment from law enforcement agencies. This audacity to challenge agribusiness and its allies in state government galvanized a whole generation of Chicano youth to join the struggle for Mexican American civil rights.[38]

The fact that Chávez picked September 16 to proclaim the strike provided a sense of historicity and linked the farmworker struggle to the Mexican Revolution of 1910, a revolution still very much a part of Mexican thought.[39] The use of a black eagle against a red background as a flag gave the farmworkers' movement an appearance of militancy, thus casting aside the stereotypic notion of the "passive" Mexican American. The NFWA was the first Mexican American organization in the latter part of the twentieth century to use music—the picket-line songs—and *teatro* to keep a sense of community and provide identity to all those who joined the struggle. Perhaps the most effective tool of the union proved to be the grape and lettuce boycotts that were launched nationally. More than any other action or use of symbolism, this boycott gave Mexican Americans everywhere a chance to become involved in *la causa* (the cause). Quickly, boycott committees working for *la causa* sprang up throughout the country, attracting Mexican Americans nationally to the cause of farmworkers' self-determination and introducing them to a new militant, working-class rhetoric.[40] In a period of peasant revolts, student mobilization, and urban guerrilla warfare worldwide, the farmworkers' movement provided a sense of solidarity between Chicano youth and liberation movements elsewhere.[41]

Chávez became the *caudillo,* the hero needed to give the struggle a national appeal. He became the first and most famous Chicano leader of the twentieth century. He was the Mexican American version of Dr. Martin Luther King. This significant point was not lost on many middle-class Mexican Americans and working-class students who were searching for a leader to rally them. From the NFWA came the Movement's eagle, *teatro,* music, and many young Chicano recruits of the picket-line wars. More important, the NFWA became a Mexican American organization much within the mainstream of its community. Unlike the middle-class organizations that sought a distance from working-class militancy and that actively attempted to gain civil rights by being "American," the NFWA lived and died on its relevance and proximity to the *comunidad.* The symbolism of the NFWA, more than its rhetoric, implied a rejection of traditional means of organizing Mexican Americans under the guise of Americanism.[42] The union came to

represent a break from the Mexican American organizations of the immediate past. Rather than a constitution, the union issued a *plan,* a traditional
Mexican declaration of grievances and plan of action; it did not seek government interference; it extolled the people's working-class roots and their
Mexicanism; and it sought to instill self-sufficiency in its members. Wel-
farism had no place in the union. Chávez would eventually move toward the
mainstream, but in the beginning he was a Mexican union man, using nationalist rhetoric to recruit farmworkers to his union and energizing thousands to work for Mexican American civil rights.

In New Mexico, the struggle for Hispano civil rights also shifted away
from the liberal agenda. There, the issues of paramount importance revolved around the ownership of the land. For decades, New Mexico Hispanos argued that their lands had been taken from them through deception
and fraud.[43] Not only were greedy landowners assailed but also the federal
government in the form of the Forest Service, which owned millions of
acres, some of them in the traditional grazing lands of northern New Mexico Hispanos. For years, Hispanos had sought judicial and legislative action
to regain the lands given to them by the Spanish crown or the Mexican government. But time and time again the reaction of state and federal officials
had been similar to the one by a representative of the U.S. State Department, who said that the claims were so "fantastic that it is difficult to form a
defense in reasonable words."[44]

When Reies López Tijerina joined the land-grant movement in 1958, he
gave new impetus to the effort. A Pentecostal preacher who received his
call when he became interested in the land-grant issue, Tijerina brought a
religious zeal to the struggle.[45] He also articulated the issue in terms of justice and civil rights. He refused to accept the slow approach. Like Chávez,
he saw the struggle in terms of right and wrong. He knew that cultural symbolism, not the Americanism of the middle-class organizations, would rally
Hispanos into a collective body. Through the Alianza Federal de Mercedes,
later to become the Alianza Federal de Pueblos Libres, Tijerina introduced
the normally conservative Hispanos of northern New Mexico to the politics of ethnicity and race. He became the first Mexican American activist
to seek out alliances with Native American and African American leaders.
First with established mainstream black leaders and eventually with black-
power advocates, Tijerina saw this partnership as a way to radicalize His-

panos into direct action, something that he saw the black community heading toward. Even before Chávez and his union became the darlings of the liberal left, Tijerina represented the radical Mexican American activist. He had the ability to radicalize the issues. Rather than allow the land-grant struggle to remain an issue between small communities, landowners, and the U.S. government, Tijerina defined the conflict as one between Mexican American and Anglo-American societies. He made cultural symbolism an important ingredient in the rallying cry by constantly reminding his followers that they were of royal lineage, recipients of kingly decrees of land. He reminded them that they had been on the land hundreds of years before the Anglo-Americans and had established institutions that predated the American conquest of the Southwest. And he did not shy away from speaking of establishing separate political entities for the Hispano, such as the Republic of San Joaquín de Chama.[46]

All of these Alianza ideals, however, were only rhetorical rejections of the liberal agenda. The real split with traditional politics came with Tijerina's legendary Tierra Amarilla raid on June 5, 1967, in which he attempted, along with more radical members of the Alianza, to make a citizen's arrest of the district attorney of Rio Arriba County.[47] A violent confrontation ensued at the Tierra Amarilla courthouse, and this led to a massive manhunt by federal, state, and county law enforcement agents. The subsequent arrest only popularized Tijerina more and made him a national celebrity in radical circles. He received invitations to speak to different groups, and he befriended black militants such as H. Rap Brown and Stokely Carmichael of the Black Panthers, as well as members of the American Indian Movement. Tijerina, now known as "El Tigre," became a model to emulate for the younger Chicano militants like Rodolfo "Corky" Gonzales of the Crusade for Justice in Colorado and José Angel Gutiérrez of the Mexican American Youth Organization (MAYO) in Texas. When he defended himself and was acquitted of the charges relating to the raid, he became an instant folk hero.[48]

To young Chicanos, awakened by the militancy of the Black Power Movement and antiwar protests, Tijerina seemed the epitome of the new Chicano leader. Whereas Chávez presented much of the cultural symbolism of the new movement, Tijerina represented the *macho,* a real man who not only talked tough but had backed up his words by taking the law into his own hands. Also, "El Tigre" reminded many of the great Mexican revolutionary heroes. He fought for land and for justice, and he called for unity among all Hispanos. If Chávez represented the man of principle, Tijerina represented the man of action. And he repudiated liberal inaction. This Chicano did not wait for liberal sensitivity or compassion; he showed that Mexican Americans were ready to move on their own.

If Chávez provided the symbolism and Tijerina symbolized direct action, then Rodolfo "Corky" Gonzales added the rhetoric and the fundamentals of an ideology that sought to distance itself from liberal moderation.[49] He also spoke for the larger urban Mexican American constituency, particularly the youth who were captivated by the activism of the times. Gonzales, a former boxer, bail bondsman, and Democratic Party activist turned militant, had been deeply involved in the war on poverty. With time, however, Gonzales became disillusioned with poverty politics and with what he perceived to be the hypocrisy of government officials. Although they spoke of helping all minorities, most of them saw only a need to be concerned with black Americans. Even when the poverty programs were sincere, Gonzales, much like Chávez and Tijerina, believed that liberal poverty programs had little to offer the poor Mexican American, especially in cities like Denver. Most of these programs did little to change the economic conditions of most Mexican Americans. They created few jobs, did not promote businesses of La Raza, and did little to rid the barrios of drugs and gangs. And they extracted a heavy price from those involved. In resigning as chairman of Denver's War on Poverty board and the Democratic Party, Gonzales accused the American political system of stripping minorities of dignity and converting them into "lackeys, political boot-lickers and prostitutes."[50] After having committed so much time and effort to working within the system, he became a "born-again" Chicano, anxious to divest himself of that which he saw as non-Mexican.

On April 29, 1966, he established the Crusade for Justice. Gonzales sought an organization that extolled the virtues of the *comunidad* by sponsoring theater productions, cultural dances, and fiestas to foster unity, as well as political discussions that promoted a self-help approach to solving problems. The Crusada became a place for the barrio people to come together and feel at home. It became particularly attractive to the young Chicanos of Denver because it was bold, rather than apologetic, and because it thrust them into the vanguard of a developing movement of rebellious Chicanos.[51] Gonzales brought a new vocabulary to the struggle, particularly the use of the term "Chicano," which in the past had been used pejoratively by many Mexican Americans and most Anglo-Americans. The term Chicano now referred to a "new" Mexican American, one who understood his or her roots and shunned assimilation or integration.

To express this new political philosophy, Gonzales wrote *I Am Joaquín/ Yo Soy Joaquín,* a poem that became the epic story of the Chicano experience.[52] It expounded what it meant to be *la gente de bronce*—a people striving to overcome oppression even as many in its ranks were attracted to the enemy's side, a people who helped build a country but could not share in its fruits, a people who faced a monumental decision in choosing between cultural genocide with slim economic benefits or cultural survival without economic benefits. The Chicano, wrote Gonzales, had chosen cultural survival over assimilation. This theme of cultural survival became a much-repeated one. Even more than Tijerina and his Hispanos, Gonzales argued that Anglo-Americans had attempted cultural genocide of Chicanos. By destroying the self-image of Chicanos, Anglo-Americans were able to rewrite history, demeaning hundreds of years of Chicano experiences. Chicanos were caught up in a social reality where they had no past; their leaders were co-opted, their lands confiscated, and their culture demeaned. They were confused in that their anger and frustration were often directed against each other in gang violence and domestic conflicts. For Chicanos, the choice seemed clear: "victory of the spirit, despite physical hunger, or . . . American social neurosis, sterilization of the soul and a full stomach."[53]

The Crusade for Justice's philosophy rejected white America in its entirety. It searched within the Chicano community for the answers to problems. To get rid of drugs and gangs from the barrio, Gonzales proposed barrio defense committees. These would also keep watch on police activity. To reduce unemployment and bring money to poor Chicano families, he proposed economic cooperatives. To develop La Raza's self-esteem, Gonzales called upon the school system to teach Mexican American history, language, and culture. The Crusade led by example, sponsoring a bilingual school that taught the history of Chicanos and numerous cultural events that promoted the barrios' artistic activities. The Crusade also established an organization called "Los Pescadores," or the Fishermen, which conducted political discussions intended to attract Chicanos to political activity. Gonzales wanted to expand Denver Chicanos' horizons by getting them involved in the farmworkers' *huelga* and by taking some of them to New Mexico to support the Alianza's efforts. It became important for Chicanos to reach out politically and culturally beyond their own barrios to others who shared similar backgrounds and faced similar problems.

Gonzales set out to revive old heroes and create new ones. Emiliano Zapata and Francisco "Pancho" Villa, of the Mexican Revolution, were exulted as examples of brave Mexicans who fought for the land rights of their poor countrymen. Fidel Castro and Che Guevara, of the Cuban Revolution, were modern-day heroes who were carrying on the century-old legacy against the "gringo" and who now inspired a new generation of Latin American revolutionaries.[54] There were also Juana Gallo, La Adelita, La Corregidora, and other women of the Mexican Revolution who formed the foundation for the "new" Chicana. They were men and women who had taken on the gringo or other oppressors and had held their own. These new heroes, as much as anything else, signaled a rejection of American political culture. No longer were young Chicanos to be taught to admire the Founding Fathers, American military heroes, or civilian elder statesmen. More important, they were taught to emulate and learn from men and women whose views were antithetical to the American political and economic system. Throughout the Movement, no organization, not even the Marxist ones, would be as scathing and bitter in its condemnation of the American way of life as the Crusade for Justice, because none ever articulated as well the perceived cultural and social genocide of the Mexican American. And except for a small number of splinter groups, no organization promoted separatism as openly as the Crusade.[55]

If the Crusade rejected Anglo values and heroes, then MAYO of Texas, and its offspring, La Raza Unida Party, condemned mainstream political and social institutions.[56] MAYO used confrontational techniques that combined racial-solidarity rhetoric and Saul Alinsky–style bombastic verbal pressure. MAYO leaders set out to personify racism in the person of the gringo, whom they defined as an Anglo racist.[57] Although the term gringo had not always carried a negative connotation, MAYO and Chicano activists promoted it as such, making it easier for Mexican Americans to focus their anger and frustrations toward one target group. After defying the enemy,

MAYO activists created the image of the Chicano social revolutionist. MAYO members were expected to put "La Raza first and foremost"; to be alert but with a closed mouth; to have a desire to study, learn, and articulate, yet be ready "to attack"; and to support fellow MAYO members in time of crisis. They were to be militant in their fight against the gringo and respectful toward La Raza, thus making them modern-day Robin Hoods. The organization was to be one made up of young Chicanos who were natural leaders willing to go back to their communities to do political organizing. Although most of the founders and initial members were students, MAYO did its best work as a community organization and not a student group. MAYO sought to identify issues important to the Mexican American community, create a grassroots group, use the politics of polarization, and eventually develop an electoral strategy.[58]

José Angel Gutiérrez, one of the founders of MAYO, argued that activists had to take advantage of the conflicts that naturally arose between Anglo-Americans and Mexican Americans over a host of issues such as poor financing of predominantly Mexican American schools; discrimination in housing and jobs; lack of political power sharing; and stereotyping of Mexican culture. He believed that Mexican Americans would respond more strongly to long, simmering dissatisfactions than to conflicts seen as coming from the outside or having no organic base. Once they identified the conflicts, these activists began work on establishing group discussions that led to the formation of community organizations based on the family structure. Providing the glue were the politics of polarization, in which the Anglo-American represented everything wrong in the lives of most Mexican Americans. Said Gutiérrez, "We felt that it was necessary to polarize the community into Chicano versus gringos. . . . After the gringo was exposed publicly, the next step was to confront his security status. . . . Once the Chicano community recognized the enemy, then he had the power to eliminate gringo attitudes by not voting for the gringo and not buying from the gringo."[59] Gutiérrez defined the gringo as a "person or institution that has a . . . policy or program . . . that reflect[s] bigotry, racism, discord . . . prejudice and violence." When asked what he meant by "eliminate the gringo," Gutiérrez responded that it would be through the removal of the base of support, be it economic, political, or social. But for Anglo-Americans the words "eliminate the gringo" would be all that they remembered, and so would most of the more angry Chicanos in the barrio. For Gutiérrez, the ambiguity and individual interpretations served the cause well.[60]

School boycotts became MAYO's most enduring trademark. The first boycotts, or "blowouts" as they were known outside of Texas, occurred in California, Colorado, and New Mexico, but it was in Texas where they proved the most effective. There were more of them in the Lone Star State than anywhere else, and they were directly or indirectly promoted by MAYO members, unlike many of the spontaneous boycotts in the other states. About thirty-nine school boycotts occurred in Texas.[61] An immediate benefit of the school boycotts was the development of student leaders, many of whom joined MAYO after seeing how successfully the organization challenged school officials. MAYO activists oriented the student leaders toward "boycott politics," assisting them in writing lists of demands, setting up press conferences, and taking control of volatile situations.

This type of educational struggle differed significantly from the one waged for decades by liberal Mexican Americans, who used the court system to strike down discriminatory statutes or practices. Their litigation and protests were meant to gain the sympathy of Anglo-American citizens and policymakers. Their efforts had been partly successful, but with time and in most school districts where Mexican American students attended, school officials learned to circumvent the law. Consequently, although de jure segregation did not exist, de facto segregation and its legacy survived in most areas. MAYO sought to challenge the legacy of segregation by demanding the institution of college preparatory courses, the establishment of culturally relevant courses, the firing of culturally biased teachers, and the elimination of the "No Spanish" rule. They also expected teachers as well as school board members to live within the local school-district area so that they would be accountable to their neighbors.[62] MAYO, however, did not believe that pressure politics would make significant changes in the schools. Only by controlling the school boards and having the power to allocate funds and make educational policy would things change permanently. This approach led to the second Crystal City revolt and the creation of La Raza Unida Party of Texas.

The politics of La Raza Unida Party were a direct affront to political liberals. Gutiérrez, as well as other Chicano activists, saw liberals as condescending and manipulative people who sought support from Mexican Americans but were unwilling to give their own support in return. Whereas conservatives were often attacked for their racism and bigotry, liberals were condemned for their "false promises" and their misuse of Mexican American loyalty. From its founding in 1970 to its demise in 1978, La Raza Unida Party waged a battle with liberal politicians for the mantel of leadership in the Mexican American community. The attack by MAYO and La Raza Unida Party on mainstream liberal and conservative politicians was intended to loosen Chicano dependence on Anglo-Americans and create space for radical ideas that emerged from the barrios. In 1974, Ramsey Muñiz, La Raza Unida Party's Texas gubernatorial candidate, told liberals that "there is no system more corrupt than a system that represents itself as the example of freedom." And to liberal Chicanos who sought the safety of the mainstream Democratic Party, he declared, "If the most you can do as a man is to crawl like a worm, you forfeit the right to protest when you get stepped on."[63]

The four organizations discussed above served as the precursors of the Chicano Movement. Their leaders provided most of the often-quoted rhetoric and the political manifestos. They were able to promote successfully a nationalist rhetoric that defined the way many Mexican Americans felt. There were other voices that also promoted a rejection of Americanism and its liberal agenda. Armando Rendón, in his much-quoted *Chicano Manifesto* (1971), described American culture as "not worth copying: it is destructive of personal dignity; it is callous, vindictive, arrogant, militaristic, self-deceiving and greedy."[64] Chicano poet Abelardo Delgado, in his poem, "Stupid America," denounced American society for limiting the intellectual and artistic growth of Chicanos:

Stupid America, hear that Chicano
shouting curses on the street
he is a poet
without paper and pencil
and since he cannot write
he will explode
. . . remember that Chicanito
flunking math and English
he is the Picasso

. . . but he will die
with one thousand masterpieces
hanging only from his lips.[65]

Even established leaders and community organizers saw a bankruptcy
in the liberal agenda and its solutions. Bert Corona, a Democrat from California who was a longtime union organizer and a past president of the Mexican American Political Association (MAPA), called on his middle-class
colleagues to endorse La Raza Unida Party and reject the two traditional
parties. Said Corona, "On the basis that these two parties [Democrats and
Republicans] have been nothing but promises—purely a love of words and
not deeds—there is only one way out, and that is to form our own party."[66]
When they did not respond, he moved away from MAPA activities and
founded CASA–Hermandad General de Trabajadores to fight for undocumented workers' rights.[67] Ernesto Galarza, a union organizer with many
years' experience working with and in the federal government, founded La
Raza Unida organization, a nonpartisan group of more militant Mexican
American middle-class activists, politicians, bureaucrats, and social workers.[68] This organization rejected the Johnson administration's efforts to
coopt the rising activism of the Chicano community in the late 1960s by
walking out of an administration-sponsored meeting in El Paso.[69] The organization refused to let the government decide who legitimately represented
the Mexican American community. It also sponsored numerous conferences that spoke to the problems of Chicanos. From the national organization, which did not remain together very long, several chapters were established in the Midwest. They eventually became social-service agencies or
advocacy groups.[70] Galarza, in his writings, called for the renewal of the
search for cultural identity. He, along with Américo Paredes of the University of Texas and Julian Samora of Notre Dame University, became intellectual mentors for many Chicano activists.[71]

María Hernández and Virginia Músquiz were longtime community activists in South Texas who also abandoned the Democratic Party and joined
La Raza Unida Party and the Chicano Movement. Unlike their male counterparts who preferred to work with middle-class organizations such as
LULAC and the American G.I. Forum, these women worked at the grassroots level, so they understood well that most things had not changed for

Chicanos in decades.[72] Young activists admired them because they were not intimidated by Anglo-American politicians or law enforcement agents. They also liked these women's attachment to the community, a characteristic perceived as of utmost importance to a community organizer.[73] In fact, MAYO activists were exhorted to go back to their communities of origin and begin to organize there. For Chicanos who were extolling the virtues of the barrio and the home community, organizers like Hernández and Músquiz represented the real organizers who never abandoned their communities.

For many of these activists, the liberal approach seemed too insignificant and too late. In a scathing letter to the editor of the newspaper *El Gallo*, the scholar Octavio Romano denounced the constant "listening" by government officials but the failure to act. In reacting to an article about Robert F. Kennedy listening to a group of Chicano students, Romano sarcastically wrote: "Oh, joy! Oh, happiness! Oh Nirvana! One more person listened. . . . Let's see now, that makes the U.S. Commission on Civil Rights . . . the secretaries of the Interior, Housing, Agriculture . . . President Johnson . . . have listened . . . people in regional offices . . . have listened . . . police departments . . . have listened, etc., etc."[74]

In rejecting the liberal agenda, these organizations and individuals interpreted the strategies of the past as having failed to arrest poverty in the barrios, to educate the children, to end discrimination, to respect the culture, or to create indigenous leadership. In fact, liberal politics had led to welfare programs, forced integration, and a perception that blacks were the only minority.[75] Chicanos came to believe that only Mexican Americans and not mainstream politicians or social workers could solve the problems of the barrio. These solutions might come with the acquiescence of the Anglo-Americans and *their* government, but it would not depend on them or their government. Mexican Americans had to take control of their lives. Unlike the Mexican American Generation, these Chicano leaders did not see the need to depend on mainstream politicians. There were to be no more "Viva Somebody" clubs or "Amigos de Someone" organizations trying to convince barrio residents to vote a certain way.[76] These activists rejected any approach that did not emphasize their unique character as a people. Chicanos looked within their community to provide answers to the persistent problems of racism, poverty, illiteracy, and political powerlessness.

Those organizations that were pro-assimilationists found it difficult to organize Mexican Americans during this period. PASSO did not survive the Movement, whereas organizations such as LULAC, the American G.I. Forum, and the National Council of La Raza eventually chose more militant leaders to help them remain viable. These new leaders, best represented by Ruben Bonilla of LULAC and Raul Yzaguirre of the National Council of La Raza, also became critical of the liberal agenda and sought a reconciliation with the community.[77] Chicano activists, as well as their moderate counterparts, realized that only through the promotion of La Raza could they expect to succeed in bringing a sense of pride and hope to the Mexican American community. And only through nationalist politics could they rally Chicanos to action. For them, the politics of the past had failed.

CHAPTER TWO

Reinterpreting the Chicano Experience

After Chicano activists rejected the liberal agenda and its prescription for integration, they set out to tackle another major obstacle to *la gente*'s progress: history. They understood that the treatment of Mexican Americans was partly the result of the distorted view of them perpetuated by historians, social scientists, essayists, and the media in general. Although Mexican American middle-class reformers had taken on many of the stereotypes, few of them had ever attempted a fundamental reinterpretation of the history of Mexican Americans.[1] They had been content with emphasizing inclusion and telling "their" side of American history. Chicano activists believed, however, that for the barrios to develop the type of self-esteem and pride necessary for political action, Mexican Americans had to see themselves in a new light. They also had to shift the blame for their condition from themselves to mainstream society. Said José Angel Gutiérrez: "We're called apathetic, disorganized. We drink beer. Like to make babies. That we fight. That we're slow learners. That we're not . . . as 'ambitiously motivated' as an Anglo. That we're weird in terms of art and music. And everything that is applied to us is really a commentary on society, the Anglo. The problem is not us. The problem is white society."[2]

To Gutiérrez and other activists, the problems of the community were most often caused by external forces. Chicanos, after all, did not create low-paying jobs, did not build inadequate housing, did not set up inefficient schools, and did not write condescending or racist advertising jingles. They also did not hire policemen with violent streaks or transport powerful drugs from South America or Asia to the barrios. These problems had been forced

upon a community that was faced with a relentless attack on its identity. Social scientists, according to Chicano activists, had continued to perpetuate
stereotypes that were destructive to the self-esteem of the Mexican American community. Chicanos who chose to read the academic literature or the
popular press came across countless references to their "apathy," "lazi-
ness," and self-victimization.[3] For many, Mexican Americans were either
emotionally or intellectually unable to lift themselves up from their difficult
conditions of poverty and illiteracy. They had been so socialized to accept
their disadvantaged status that it had become part of the culture. This culture of poverty, argued social scientists, provided few, if any, of the tools to
help Mexican Americans pull themselves out of the cycle of hopelessness in
which they were caught.[4]

Chicanos also saw themselves as victims of history, though they did
not see culture as at fault. Luis Valdez, founder of the Teatro Campesino,
saw Mexican Americans as being treated as, and consequently acting like,
a "colonized race . . . [whose] uniqueness . . . lies buried in the dust of conquest." The conquest had been not only a military one but a psychological
one, since Mexican Americans had been cut off from their history.[5] The solution to this condition, according to Valdez, was to "reach into our people,
into the . . . memory of their beginning."[6] Chicanos had to find a past un-
marred by the conquest, and within that past find the prototype society
where the early "Chicano" was unspoiled by Anglo-American society. David
Sánchez, prime minister of the paramilitary group the Brown Berets, described it thus: "In the beginning . . . there were beautiful lands with all the
living resources. . . . It was a paradise where the balance of nature kept
everyone alive. . . . We were a proud people who perfected medicines . . .
until strange ships came from an old world. . . . They came not to build, but
to rule . . . at the cost of our blood."[7]

In that past, Chicanos searched for a reinterpretation of their existence
that would uncover the myths and legends of the struggle for survival and
provide the basis for a cultural and political renaissance. This new interpretation of the Chicano experience also sought to undo the years of biased
scholarship that formed the core of what was known about the Mexican
American. In 1968, Enriqueta Longeaux y Vásquez wrote: "The raza in the
southwest . . . wants our history back. . . . Our cities, our mountains, and
rivers were explored and settled by Indians and Spaniards, not pilgrims and

wagon masters. The first cattle raisers, cowboys and farmers were raza. We weren't waiting here to be saved by the great white fathers."[8]

Octavio Romano was one of the first Chicano scholars to promote the new interpretation. An anthropologist at the University of California, Berkeley, he attacked much of the traditional scholarship on Mexican Americans by social scientists. In his most influential article, "The Anthropology and Sociology of the Mexican-American: The Distortion of Mexican-American History," Romano took on the academy: "Social science studies have dealt with Mexican Americans as an ahistoric people—with a place in history reserved for them only when they undergo some metamorphosis usually called acculturation. . . . Mexican Americans are never seen as participants in history, much less as generators of the historical process."[9] For activists, Chicano history was a recollection of events, of ideas, and of people who had resisted the American conquest of the Southwest and the subsequent colonization that followed. They believed that to "deprive man of his heritage was the worst form of oppression."[10] So they set out to uncover facts long forgotten or ignored and to debunk the Anglo-American version of their history. To do so required more than a different retelling, it meant framing the discovered history within a new interpretation that challenged the traditional literature. This interpretation presented Chicanos as active participants in "their" history.

Romano chided social scientists who wrote that Mexican Americans had a difficult time dealing with the conflict between the two cultures. This conflict, one anthropologist argued, often led them to "retreat" into their "conservative . . . world," to "escape to larger cities" or into alcoholism, or to engage in antisocial behavior. Their only hope rested on their acculturating "more and more."[11] Although offended by the belittling descriptions of Mexican Americans, Romano reacted more angrily to the implication that only acculturated Mexican Americans were active participants in their lives. Romano rebutted, "Contrary to the ahistorical views . . . Mexican Americans as well as Mexican immigrants have not . . . wallowed passively in some teleological treadmill, awaiting the emergence of an acculturated third generation before joining in the historical process."[12] He cited numerous instances when Mexican Americans had engaged in strikes in the agricultural fields and the mines of eight different states. These had been intense, even violent acts of labor resistance that had incurred a "massive counter-action" that included widespread deportations. Romano pointed to Carey McWilliams, who wrote in 1949: "Long charged with a lack of 'leadership' and talent for organization, they proved all too effectively that neither talent was lacking. . . . By 1930 the myth of the docility of Mexican labor had been thoroughly exploded."[13]

Romano took on the anthropologist Ruth Tuck, who in 1946 wrote: "For many years the (Mexican) immigrant and his sons made no effort to free themselves. They burned with resentment over a thousand slights, but they did so in private. . . . Perhaps this passivity is the mark of any minority which is just emerging."[14] With that statement, said Romano, Tuck wiped away decades of resistance and set a tone for anthropologists and sociologists to emulate in describing Mexican Americans and their condition. Romano then took on Munro Edmonson, Celia Heller, Julian Samora, Lyle Saunders, and others whose works only reaffirmed Tuck's conceptualization of the Mexican American as a victim of his or her cultural deficiencies.[15] In summarizing their work, Romano accused the aforementioned scholars of making Mexican Americans the generators of their problems, thus freeing Anglo-Americans from most responsibility. Calling upon his readers to reject these perceptions of traditional Mexican culture, he urged them to learn about the intellectual history of Mexican Americans.

That led to another important article, "The Historical and Intellectual Presence of Mexican Americans."[16] Although not as influential as his first one, this article sought to provide a picture of the pluralistic nature of the Mexican American community and to point out that there were important philosophical and ideological currents that influenced the thinking of most Mexican Americans. Romano posited that three main streams of thought permeated the Mexican American community. These were "indianist philosophy," "historical confrontation," and "cultural nationalism." "At times," wrote Romano, "they [the three philosophies] coincide with actual historical occurrences. Other times they lie relatively dormant, or appear in a poetic metaphor, a song, a short story told to children, or in a marriage pattern."[17] Indianist philosophy dealt with the indigenous origin of most Mexican Americans; historical confrontation dealt with protest and popular action against tyranny and oppression; and cultural nationalism concerned itself with the development of the cultural characteristics of being a *mexicano*.

These philosophies came from the Mexican Revolution, an event that

Romano believed influenced most Mexicans who crossed the border at the turn of the century. The philosophies were passed on from generation to generation and remained an active intellectual element within an extremely diverse community. These philosophies were responsible for the resistance that Chicanos continually waged against opposition. They were also responsible for the nationalistic or ethnocentric response of the working class toward Anglo-American encroachment into their community. Romano concluded his article by warning Chicanos to avoid being "permanently entombed in the histories of the past."[18] As a young recruit to the Movement, I read Romano's first article and felt outraged over the academic scholarship on Mexican Americans. It became a hotly discussed and debated article in my "Introduction to Mexican Americans" course at Texas A & I University in Kingsville. It would be quoted over and over in Chicano newspapers, lectures, and rallies, and in other academic articles and papers during the early years of the Movement.[19] Romano had, in a few short pages, identified what most Chicano activists perceived to be the most damaging assault on the Mexican American community. Said Romano, "Mexican Americans are [seen as] simple-minded . . . children who . . . choose poverty and isolation instead of assimilating into the American mainstream."[20]

The teaching of such perceptions had served to perpetuate stereotypes and thus kept mainstream society unsympathetic and often hostile toward Mexican Americans. The racist feelings and remarks had, in part, been rationalized by liberal social scientists who saw Mexican Americans as passive, unmotivated, and responsible for accepting much of their own suffering.[21] The biased scholarship had also served to perpetuate feelings of inferiority among many Mexican Americans and to cause some of the more educated to remove themselves culturally and physically from their communities. For me, and many like me, the article revealed a condescending attitude by social scientists who—we believed—would not have written about blacks in the same manner. We were under the impression that blacks, through the civil-rights movement, were freed from much of this type of scholarship. It was a false assumption but one that led many of us to the next phase of our politicalization. Although we were always conscious of discrimination, many of us often abdicated the role of "oppressed minority" to blacks because few of us had ever understood the extent of the discrimination and racism perpetrated against Mexican Americans. To find that

Mexican Americans were also victims of intellectual racism, and then to realize that there was no civil-rights movement for Mexican Americans, made many of us anxious to get involved in a movement of our own. The seeming lack of Anglo-American sympathy caused the Chicano Movement to become more nationalistic and separatist in nature than it might have been.[22]

Following Romano's lead, many other Chicano college students and professors picked up the discussion of the portrayal of Mexican Americans in the academic and popular literature. Juan Gómez-Quiñones, a young scholar at the University of California at Los Angeles at the time, called for a reconceptualization of Mexican American history, arguing that the history of Chicanos was not simply a history of the "Anglo oppressor" and the "Chicano oppressed."[23] He attempted to construct the first framework for retelling the story of the Mexican American. In an article entitled "Notes on Periodization, 1900–1965," Gómez-Quiñones broke Mexican American history into several definable periods.[24] Carlos Muñoz, a graduate student at the University of California, called on Chicanos scholars and students to be more than academicians. The Chicano scholar, said Muñoz, "must commit himself to the emancipation of his people."[25] Journals such as *Aztlan, De Colores, Caracol, Regeneración, Encuentro Femenil,* and Romano's *El Grito* followed the lead of these writers and charged ahead with a scathing scholarship that sought to disprove stereotypes that had become part of the mainstream in academia.[26] All of the aforementioned were academic journals with the exception of *Caracol,* which was a popular magazine for the masses that published a hodgepodge of articles, poems, theater acts, and essays.[27] These and other periodicals became self-imposed required reading for college students and Chicano activists in the community. Whereas many Chicanos were attracted to the Movement by the rhetoric and passion of the leaders, others less passionate were attracted by the intellectual discourse on the status of Chicanos, their past, and what might lie ahead. For many students coming to universities with little knowledge of their past, it became an intellectual culture shock to read the new Chicano scholarship.[28]

If Romano's article began the debate, Rodolfo Acuña's *Occupied America* heightened its intensity. No other academic work caused the controversy that Acuña's history of Chicanos did. Beginning with the premise that Chicanos were an internal colony still suffering from the legacy of the American conquest, Acuña went on to describe in detail many of the atrocities committed against La Raza. He introduced the book in this manner: "*Occupied America* has evolved from my belief that the history of Chicanos . . . must be reexamined. . . . As my research progressed, I became convinced that the experiences of Chicanos in the United States parallel that of other Third World people who have suffered under the colonialism of technologically superior nations. Thus, the thesis of this monograph is that Chicanos . . . are a colonized people. The conquest of the Mexicans, the occupation of their land and the continued oppression they have faced document this thesis."[29]

For Chicano activists, Acuña's work was a godsend. No longer did they have to piece together accounts of discrimination and racism. In several hundred pages, Acuña documented more than enough incidents to confirm almost anything that activists chose to blame on American society.[30] Chicano academicians also quickly endorsed the book because it provided them with a text for their courses. In it they found a comprehensive and panoramic view of Chicano history. Its model of "internal-colonialism" also provided a framework by which to explain the Chicano experience. The internal-colony model posited that the Southwest had been subjected to a conquest and a ruthless process of colonization that left Mexican Americans in circumstances similar to those of nations that had been colonized by imperialist powers. A dual-wage system, rampant segregation, exploitation of natural resources, coaptation of the native elites, and other characteristics of a foreign colony were present in the Southwest, according to Acuña. The internal-colony social structure also placed racial conflict at the center of Mexican and Anglo-American relationships.[31] Chicano students were immediately attracted to the book by the information, much of it new to them, and by its academic "legitimacy." They also liked its militancy. Far from being esoteric, it invited the reader to action, to be an active participant in history. It also provided heroes and heroines and allowed Chicano students to see that Mexican Americans had never been passive. Rather, they had resisted domination. In a time of lettuce and grape boycotts, land-grant battles, urban street militancy, and school walkouts, *Occupied America* became the intellectual bible that rationalized the heightened militancy.

In Acuña's account of the conquest of the Southwest, nothing had come by chance, or by a spontaneous desire by Anglo-American settlers to live free under a democratic government. Instead, these settlers, in collusion with merchants, land speculators, businessmen, and government officials, had plotted to take Mexico's land. "Remember the Alamo" was not the defiant cry of a ragtag army of freedom-loving men but that of a band of ruffians and outlaws who had come to Texas to engage in their own brand of frontier conquest. Acuña, in this short monograph, rewrote the histories of Texas, Arizona, California, and New Mexico, documenting the methods used to conspire for revolution and war as well as how, once attaining victory, these invaders conspired to steal the lands from the Mexicans who had chosen to stay behind. In Acuña's account there were no tough, democratically inclined cowboys who tamed the West with courage, integrity, and a single six-gun. Instead, Acuña painted a picture of fraud, violence, and lawlessness—of a time when all Mexican possessions were an open target; when the law was exclusively on the side of the Anglo-Americans; and when a heterogeneous Mexican society had, for the most part, been violently compressed into a powerless, poor rural caste. But Mexicans and their Chicano offspring fought back, wrote Acuña. In California, social bandits such as Joaquín Murrieta and Tiburcio Vásquez fought violence with violence of their own. In New Mexico, "Las Gorras Blancas" cut the wire fences of land-grabbing land barons, and the Partido del Pueblo Unido fought the Anglo-American political machines in the electoral arena. In Texas, *revolucionarios* such as Catarino Garza and Juan Cortina led several uprisings against the landed and urban elites in South Texas. The battles against the Texas Rangers and the union strikes in the mines of Arizona and the pecan factories in San Antonio became part of the border mythology. The Mexican American community had finally succumbed to oppression, but these men and numerous women became heroes through Acuña's book.

In his concluding chapter, Acuña reaffirmed the prevailing rejection of American society articulated by the leaders of the emerging movement: "Chicanos who actively participated in the political life of the nation took a hard look at their assigned role in society, evaluated it, and then decided that they had had enough, so they bid goodbye to America."[32] In this chapter, Acuña depicted the rise of a new generation of leaders who had lost hope of finding solutions through the traditional channels of protest and litigation. Although the book ended on a somber, almost pessimistic note, Acuña nonetheless succeeded in setting the tone for the intense struggle for Chicano liberation. No other book before or since has carried the pow-

erful message that Mexican Americans are an exploited and oppressed minority but one that has fought and continues to fight back.

I would never look at American society in the same way after reading
Occupied America. For many like myself, our historical roots had been torn
from the American soil, and we set out in a quest to find identity and to
learn history—"our" history. Romano and Acuña led the search for more
Chicano history. The new heroes became those who resisted the American
conquest of the Southwest. Mexican military men who fought against the
Texas rebels or who defended Mexico against the American invasion became men to admire. Particularly admirable were men like Catarino Garza
and Juan Cortina, who rose up in arms to defend their Mexican compatri-
ots. As inspiring were Emma Tenayuca, who led the pecan shellers' strike
in San Antonio in the 1930s, and Luisa Moreno, an organizer for the United
Cannery, Agricultural, and Packing Workers of America and a founder of El
Congreso de los Pueblos de Habla Español in 1938.[33] The search for heroes
did not end with larger-than-life men and women. With time, our heroes became those individuals who survived the daily struggles in a society still
foreign to them.

Romano and Acuña were not the only ones writing this new interpretation. After the initial attack on the Anglo-American academy, Chicano scholars began to write their own history. Gómez-Quiñones wrote about the
labor struggles of Chicanos and their early political activism. And he provided an in-depth view of the first ideological hero of the Chicano Movement when he wrote a biography of Ricardo Flores Magón, the Mexican anarchist and intellectual precursor of the Mexican Revolution. For the more
ideological radicals in the Movement, Magón became and remained the
most influential historical figure in Mexican history.[34] Gómez-Quiñones
also pioneered the field of Chicano studies and served as a mentor for many
graduate students who wrote about Chicanos in the pages of *De Colores,
Aztlan, El Grito,* and other academic journals. His influence, through his
writings and the students he mentored, was felt strongly in California and
on college campuses nationwide. There were others. Renato Rosaldo promoted Mexican American studies at the University of Arizona and compiled
the work *Chicanos: The Beginnings of Bronze Power,* one of the first anthologies of articles on Mexican Americans produced by a major publisher. Al-
berto Camarillo wrote about urban Chicanos in California; Américo Paredes

and José Limon wrote about folklore, *corridos,* and the Rio Grande Valley; Emilio Zamora wrote about Chicano socialist activists at the turn of the century; Margarita Melville, Adelaida del Castillo, and other women scholars wrote about Chicanas in labor, politics, and letters. Anglo-American scholars such as Stan Steiner, Joan C. Moore, and David Weber also wrote works relevant to the study of Chicanos. Still others involved in this work were amateur historians, many of them poets, dramatists, and artists who incorporated history within their art. Each of them sought to reinterpret history and to create the necessary heroes, heroines, and myths needed to add flames to the Chicano cultural renaissance. Social scientists could not fill the void on the Chicano experience fast enough, so many essayists and fiction writers contributed to the reinterpretation.

These new writers created an image of themselves and their people that did not integrate into mainstream society. In the past, Mexican American writers had struggled to force themselves into the American literary mainstream. Most wrote of their people and themselves as marginalized individuals awaiting the acculturation of their community. Marcienne Rocard has written of the contrast between these two generations: "The older Mexican American poets and short-story writers were isolated; though they sometimes attacked the dominant society harshly and felt themselves to be marginal, they were part of it in spite of themselves. They had no separate image of themselves. By contrast, Chicano writers had a will to define and assert themselves with respect to the Anglo world, a will conditioned by ethnic allegiance."[35] They were, she added, obsessed with identity.

While historians sought to discover the history of Chicanos and sociologists worked to correct the stereotypes, Chicano writers attempted to give meaning to the Chicano experience by blending the social science with folklore and mythmaking. They were at times historians, social critics, seers, and political cheerleaders. More than anyone else, Chicano writers created, expanded, and exported their "new" history as they traveled throughout the barrios of the Southwest reading their works.[36] Their topics ranged from the Aztec gods to the Mexican Revolution; from the *pachuco* to the migrant farmworker; and from the young Chicano militants to Che Guevara, Augusto Sandino, Lucio Cabañas, and Fidel Castro. Most of the poetry dealt with identity and pride in being Chicano.[37] Poetry took the Chicano mind where history could not. Whereas historians wrote of brave men and women who resisted oppression, and of short-lived victories against the Anglo-American, poems provided the ultimate victory. In them, history and the present were described not as they were but as they could and would become. It was in the realm of literature that Chicanos had full control of their lives. There were no facts to contradict Chicano liberation. In poetry Anglo-Americans were simpletons; policemen cowardly; American culture degenerate; and Chicanos organic, brave intellectuals with a rich and moral culture.[38]

Art was another form of history, since most of it depicted the Chicano's Indian heritage and the community's legacy of struggle. Many Mexican American children first learned about Pancho Villa, Emiliano Zapata, Benito Juárez, Cuauhtémoc, and other Mexican heroes from the murals in the barrio. Art was another form that transcended historical facts and provided a new view of La Raza. The murals were larger than life, and the people in them could not help but be seen as heroic. Much of the impetus for this "new" art came from the Mexican revolutionary muralists like Diego Rivera and David Alfaro Siqueiros.

Probably as important as the poetry and art was Chicano *teatro*. With the founding of the Teatro Campesino at the start of the farmworkers' struggle in the mid-1960s, theater became an important tool in the development of identity and militancy. In the case of Teatro Campesino, as well as other Chicano theater groups, the playwright and the actors were part of the social movement. Their topics were usually discrimination, racism, police brutality, workers on strike, or Chicano culture. The goal went beyond entertainment. Theater became a way by which people came to terms with their condition. The tradition of *teatro* in the barrio had been an entrenched one up until about the 1950s. Traveling theater troupes called *carpas,* whose name referred to the tents under which they performed, were a common feature in the Mexican American communities of the Southwest.[39] The skits were usually satires that presented a working-class view of the world. It made gentle fun of people in the barrio, while being particularly cutting toward middle- and upper-class *sociedad.* Props and scenery were kept to a minimum, and most skits were improvised. Few were political in a partisan or ideological way, but they nonetheless provided commentary on people's lives. For parents, these *variedades* (variety shows)[40] were a way to keep their children immersed in the culture and to strengthen their language skills in Spanish. It was also a way to keep the family together, because parents understood that American culture and the public schools were pulling their children away from them. The theater groups kept them close to their culture and *patria*. Although some parents had left Mexico willingly and had no desire to return, they nevertheless felt estranged from their country, and the *carpas* provided some relief from the alienation that they felt in the United States.[41]

Chicano theater groups emulated many aspects of the early Mexican troupes. They were not particularly ideological as much as they were critical of American society. In its early development, Chicano theater proved to be more critical of Anglo-American culture and of those Mexican Americans who sought assimilation than of the political system. With time that changed, and the country's policies at home and abroad became the targets of Chicano satire. Its most significant function, however, remained its promotion of the "new" Chicanos.

Teatro Campesino served as the model for most of these Chicano theater groups. Founded in 1965, it sought to teach farmworkers about the union activities of César Chávez and to attract them to union membership. In 1972, Luis Valdez, the Teatro's founder, wrote the following about its use of skits and funny scenes to further *la causa*: "Our use of comedy stemmed from necessity—the necessity of lifting the strikers' morale. We found we could make social points [commentary] not in spite of the comedy, but through it. Slapstick can bring us . . . close to the underlying tragedy . . . that human beings have been wasted for generations."[42] For two years after its founding, Teatro Campesino worked alongside the union in the picket lines. Its actors performed in the fields, in the labor camps, at rallies, at union meetings, and at strike benefits. They also toured the country and at each stop publicized the union boycotts, informing Mexican American and Anglo-American audiences about the plight of the farmworkers. They advocated a rural culturalism that sought to tie all Chicanos to the land. This culturalism promoted the family as the unit of struggle, since in farmworker families everyone worked in the fields to help out. Once unionized, all members of the family became connected to the strike, boycott, or picket line. For Teatro Campesino there existed a new Chicano, willing to work for *la causa*. This Chicano shunned materialism and looked to the land and his or her history for meaning.

The founders of Teatro Campesino, as well as those of the union, knew there existed another kind of Mexican American. He was the *vendido,* the Mexican American willing to sell out his people to the highest bidder. In the rural areas he was the Mexican labor contractor, in the urban barrios he was the *politico,* and at the university he was the acculturated Chicano who believed in the system and in education for the professional advantages it brought. The theater became the place to expose this type of character, and thus the *vendido* became one of the stock characters of most Chicano plays. It was the United Farm Workers Union (UFW)[43] that first identified the dichotomy within the Chicano community. Union organizers quickly labeled as "sell-outs" those Mexican Americans who were afraid to challenge the growers or those who worked for them. In identifying a character such as the *vendido,* Chicano theater provided a contrast for the new Chicano. It also was a way to belittle and discredit those who straddled the fence or sided against the Movement. In time, it became a way to keep discipline within the ranks, since the threat of being designated a *vendido* intimidated many a wavering Chicano activist.[44]

Chicano theater groups appeared throughout the Southwest. The Crusade for Justice had its own theater group, and so did many other organizations. But although they were supportive of the Movement, most Chicano theater groups were independent of control from activists. This freedom gave them the ability to transcend local or regional issues and allowed them artistic freedom. Much as in the Chicano Movement, their ideological base resulted from a hodgepodge of ideas and concerns. The underlying theme of all of their work, and the one with which all Chicanos could identify, was the threat of cultural genocide and its economic, social, and spiritual legacy. The *teatros* provided a simple message: Chicanos and their culture were under attack; they had to resist by knowing their history and maintaining their culture and they had to root out the *vendidos* from among them. That theme served Chicano activists from the California college campuses to the migrant shanty towns of Hidalgo County in Texas. Chicano theater, much like Chicano literature, provided a more positive view of the Mexican American community. Although the history and experience depicted in the plays often defied historical accuracy, they nevertheless projected a positive image and created new myths, something of which Chicanos seemed so much in need.

Two other institutions promoted a new interpretation of the Chicano experience: Chicano studies programs and centers, and the Chicano press. Both Chicano studies, as a political and academic movement, and the Chicano press, as a conveyor of information, proved to be crucial to the reinterpretation of the Chicano experience. More Chicanos learned about "their" history and about brown militancy from these two institutions than from any other source. Their importance to the Movimiento cannot be overemphasized.

Chicano studies programs began appearing on college campuses in the mid-1960s in response to student demands that Mexican American history and culture be taught as part of the academic curriculum. These programs first appeared in California as a result of the student strikes occurring in Los Angeles and other major cities. The main impetus for the growth of Chicano studies, however, came from a conference at the University of California at Santa Barbara in April 1969. There, over one hundred delegates from 29 campuses met under the sponsorship of the Chicano Coordinating Committee on Higher Education to develop a master plan for Chicanos in higher education.[45]

In El Plan de Santa Barbara, which came out of the conference and became the Movement's design for educating the Chicano masses, the authors declared: "We recognize that without a strategic use of education that places value on what we value, we will not realize our destiny. . . . Throughout history the quest for cultural expression and freedom has taken the form of a struggle."[46] This "strategic use of education" meant Chicano students and faculty were to be involved in the development of curriculum and in the administration of programs. It also meant that these programs would be within what Carlos Muñoz called "the context of a politics for change."[47] The Plan's authors express this context in the following manner: "Now Chicano university students, not unmindful of the historic price of assimilation, take change within the community as the point of departure for their social and political involvement. . . . At this moment we do not come to work for the university, but to demand that the university work for our people."[48] Many of those hired to teach and direct the programs used the classroom to expound their version of Chicano history. For those who found themselves in areas where there were no major Movement organizations, the courses in Chicano studies allowed them to participate, at least emotionally, in the Movement. Also, many of these programs sponsored trips to large protest activities, marches, and militant conferences.

In Kingsville, many joined the Movement through the efforts of José Reyna, head of the Ethnic Studies program at Texas A & I University. In his classroom, students read Romano's articles, Acuña's book, and the countless other articles, books, and periodicals that were surfacing during the early 1970s. Self-identity usually became the main topic of the courses offered there and in other places. In class environments made up mostly of Chicanos, students often discussed and debated issues that would have been deemed inappropriate in other classrooms.[49] In places such as California State University at Northridge, degrees were offered in Chicano studies, and students graduating from these programs were expected to have some fluency in both Spanish and Náhuatl (the language of the Aztecs) and to know their Mexican and Chicano history. In other places, like Kingsville, where lack of university support limited the programs, students were provided the basics of Chicano thought and were then exhorted to join community grassroots organizations that were involved in some form of activism. The Chicano studies programs provided a sense of legitimacy for many and a place in which Chicano intellectual debates were appreciated.[50] It was also for many a place where the correct "history" of La Raza could be learned. According to an editorial in *El Grito,* "The responsibility upon the shoulders of those in Chicano programs is great, for should the end product be disfigured in any way whatsoever, they will have turned victory into defeat, self-expression into self-denial, a dream into a nightmare, and a promise into . . . purposeless mouthings."[51] For Chicano academicians, Chicano studies programs were a personal responsibility. They sought to eliminate "past distortions." The "future image" was now in their hands, and they set out to craft that image.[52]

Through the efforts of Chicano studies and ethnic studies programs, many Chicanos rediscovered their culture, learned about their history, and regained an identity many had lost or had never acquired at home. Through these programs, students participated in local community activities such as Diez y Seis de Septiembre and Cinco de Mayo celebrations (Mexican patriotic holidays) and local elections and protests. It was not uncommon for groups associated with a Chicano studies program to sponsor Christmas parties, food drives, or picnics for the local Chicano community.[53] Students

who had often been unaware of cultural events in their hometowns, or who
had simply not been interested in participating, now became involved. With
the mentoring of their professors, they saw the community in a different
light. Herbal remedies, cultural traditions, and other barrio survival techniques became symbols of resistance to an alienating urban world. No
longer were students ashamed of the cure-all *hierbas,* the *parteras,* the *salsa
picante* and *tacos,* the *quinceañeras,* and other cultural "anomalies" in which
the barrio participated. Rather than blame La Raza for its poverty, dropout
rates, or juvenile delinquency, many college students, tutored by their Chicano instructors, shifted the blame to mainstream Anglo-American society.
Chicano culture became all good, healthy, and moral; problems encountered
were those that had been inflicted on the barrios by external forces. For
many Chicano students, the Chicano experience took on a different character than even the one they had experienced themselves. Isolated in a university environment often foreign to them, they saw the community as warm
and familiar. Although they were in reality separated by education and status from the community, they felt a greater connection to it than ever before. Nostalgia had become history.

For those who did not attend the university, the Chicano press served
as the catalyst for intellectual discussion. "*El Gallo* was born out of frustration and determination for the truth," wrote "Corky" Gonzales of the Crusade's newspaper, in 1967.[54] One year later, the editors of *El Grito del Norte*
would declare their intent to promote the "course of justice of the poor people . . . and conserve the cultural heritage of la raza."[55] Chicano newspapers
carried bits of history, literature, current news, commentary, and a strong
dose of cultural polemics.

There were three kinds of newspapers and magazines that formed the
nucleus of the Chicano press. The first were newspapers that represented
specific organizations and usually promoted particular political philosophies. There were the UFW's *El Malcriado,* La Raza Unida Party's *Para la
Gente,* the Brown Berets' *Regeneración,* the newspapers of other major Chicano Movement groups, and other smaller periodicals representing smaller
organizations. These were initially the most influential and most scathing
in their polemics. The second category of newspapers included those
published by university student groups. These were mostly disseminated
within the local university community and to other college campuses

throughout the country. These newspapers dealt with issues of academic freedom, Chicano studies, and student politics and published a fair amount of commentary on international issues. They were often the most brash and used language deemed inappropriate for the other two categories of newspapers. Some of these were *El Chile* from Texas A & I University at Kingsville and *El Chingazo* from San Diego State University. The third kind of publication was the independent newspapers directed toward the community, even though some came from university groups or particular partisan groups. These periodicals tended to publish for a longer period of time and were as popular outside the locality where they were published as they were within. Examples were *El Grito del Norte* from Denver; *La Raza* from Los Angeles; and *Caracol* from San Antonio, Texas.

These news sheets were in essence the wire service for Chicano activists throughout Aztlán. Articles that originated in the pages of these periodicals were reprinted in other newspapers, duplicated, and passed out during rallies or political discussions. This kept the flow of ideas going and bound all of the peripheries to the centers of Chicano activism. Through them, Chicanos learned what issues were of greatest importance to the greatest number of Chicanos. From them also came word as to which leaders were rising in the Movement and which were fading. Much like radio and television for American society, the Chicano press developed a "mainstream" image of what a Chicano or Chicana in the Movement did or said.

None of the aforementioned periodicals, nor most of the others, had rigid ideological lines to present. They were nationalistic, anticapitalist, and geared toward action. *El Grito del Norte* tended to concentrate on the work of the Alianza, *El Gallo* on the politics of the Crusade for Justice, and *La Raza* on the California activities of the Chicano student movement and later La Raza Unida Party. *Caracol* tended to be the most independent. It also became the most diversified, with over half of its pages devoted to poems, autobiographical essays, plays, and short stories. These newspapers and magazines provided a view of local, national, and international events from a Chicano perspective. The war in Vietnam was important in relation to how many Chicanos were being killed. The national liberation movements in Asia, Africa, and Latin America were analyzed to identify strategies that Chicanos could use in their own liberation. And American foreign policy received critical scrutiny to confirm the Chicano condemnation of American imperialism. Locally, the coverage revolved around daily occurrences of discrimination; local laws, ordinances, or practices that treated Chicanos as second-class citizens; and political victories by community groups.[56]

The periodicals evolved politically with time. Most went from covering the local community to commenting on national and international events. As time went by, and political victories at home became more difficult to obtain, the newspapers increased their polemical discussions on ideology and "Yankee imperialism." They also moved away from cultural events and histories that had been the mainstay of the first issues. Nevertheless, the newspapers remained the promoters of the new image of the Chicano. And they continued to interpret the Chicano experience in a separatist mode, where aggression and resistance were the main themes of that experience. Some of these newspapers later made the transition to becoming community newspapers, while others spurned more traditional periodicals that were in business to make money and not political commentary.

By the mid-1970s, for those who took time to notice, Chicanos had created a historical image for themselves. This image of a historical people with heroes, legends, intellectual foundations, and culture differed dramatically from that which came from the academic and popular literature. Mexican Americans no longer had to accept the view of the Chicano as a lazy, unambitious, violent individual with insatiable sexual desires and a culture that bred poverty and delinquency. They also did not have to accept the image of passivity. This new outlook became important as Chicano activists rejected the liberal approach to solving the problems of the community. A failure to replace the image of the nonachieving Chicano at a time when the liberal approach was rejected would have meant that Chicanos were worse off than they believed. When they had been unable to develop a mass protest movement, the liberal approach had been a safety net for Mexican Americans. The piecemeal approach had had its benefits. Once that approach was rejected, Chicanos needed a stronger self-image in order to embark on their own program of self-help. Historical identity became crucial for activists. This identity developed through the efforts of academicians, who rejected stereotypes and dug out the real history; poets and playwrights, who presented culturally militant Chicanos and Chicanas as the prototypes of the new Mexican American; Chicano studies programs, which involved students and created a reservoir of Chicano intellectuals; and newspapers and magazines, which kept Chicanos informed of what was happening in Aztlán and which served to develop a cultural and political "homogeneity" among Chicano activists.[57] The reinterpretation of the Chicano experience affected the way particular sectors within the Chicano community saw themselves. Even in segments of the community where radicalism did not dominate the mode of operations, the new view of Chicanos caused considerable change. The Church—as used here, denoting religious groups within the community, predominantly the Catholic Church—was one such entity deeply affected by the Chicano Movement's activism and its interpretation of history.[58]

For many Chicano activists, the Church had been one of those institutions that had cooperated in the oppression of the Chicano masses by teaching them subserviency and by encouraging them to be happy with their lot on Earth, as heaven would bring celestial rewards.[59] For others, the Church represented a financial and social power that refused to intervene on behalf of the poor Chicano. "The religious dollar must be invested, without return expected, in the barrios," declared an editorial in *El Grito del Norte*.[60] César Chávez, a man of deep religious loyalty, also called for a more sensitive Church. "It is our duty" to appeal to the church for the poor, he told readers of *El Grito* in 1968. "It should be as natural as appealing to government . . . and we do that often enough."[61] The Mexican American Youth Organization (MAYO) had even responded to the Church's passivity with sacrilege in 1969 when its members spray-painted brown a statue of Our Lady of the Immaculate Conception that stood on the grounds of an old seminary building in Mission, Texas. They had done so to protest the Church's refusal to give them the building for their "university without walls" and for its overall lack of support for the Movement.[62] Other activists who were Marxist-oriented, or disciples of anarchy, saw the Church as reactionary.

There were others, however, who saw that the Church was an important institution in the barrio and that many Mexican Americans remained faithful to it. "God is alive and well in the heart of the Chicano," Luis Valdez would write during the height of the grape and lettuce boycott.[63] They also saw within it a number of Chicano and Anglo-American priests ready to join the Movement. While preaching against the Church's hierarchy, many activists united with lay leaders and clergy to promote Movement activities. In New Mexico, Reies López Tijerina, a former Pentecostal preacher, would lead the land-grant movement with a religious zeal and place it within the context of a spiritual crusade. In Robstown, Texas, a number of the early Movement candidates were Baptist lay leaders. At Brigham Young University, a Chicano from San Antonio's Spanish-speaking Mormon congregation established the university's first ethnic studies club. In Tucson, a Methodist parish provided the meeting space for the Mexican American Liberation Committee. And in New York, Protestant churches, responding to lay leaders' demands, established the National Farm Workers Ministry.[64]

Chávez was the most adept at using the Church as a powerful ally. In the UFW union hall in Delano, California, a large banner reminded the farmworkers daily that "God is beside you on the picket line." In rallying the poor Chicanos to continue their strikes and their organizing amid arrests, intimidation, and seemingly unbeatable odds, Chávez continually used religious symbolism and rhetoric to inspire his followers. The march to Sacramento became a religious pilgrimage. "They [the farmworkers] hope to set themselves at peace with the Lord, so that the justice of their cause will be purified of all lesser motivations."[65] The fasts became petitions for "nonviolence and a call to sacrifice." They also became a way to attract national attention to the nobleness of the cause. For the UFW, the Virgen de Guadalupe became the patron saint of the Movement, accompanying its strikers on the picket lines, marches, and rallies. Organizations such as Católicas por La Raza, PADRES, HERMANAS, and other arose.[66]

Movement activists learned to acknowledge that religious affiliation remained important for many Mexican Americans. To make that affiliation beneficial for the Movement meant reinterpreting the Church's historical role in the community. To do so, these activists looked back in history to find those religious leaders who had sided with the oppressed and the Indians. They found Fathers Miguel Hidalgo y Costilla and José María Morelos y Pavón of the Mexican War for Independence, and they found religious revolutionaries such as Ruben Jaramillo, a lay Methodist preacher, who fought alongside the famous Mexican peasant leader of the Revolution of 1910, Emiliano Zapata. Others simply reinterpreted the role of Christ, making him a revolutionist. "For it is from him that we draw our strength," said an activist calling herself Dolores del Grito.[67] Tijerina would compare his actions to those of an angry god: "The revolution of Tierra Amarilla was like Christ entering the temple and clearing out the Pharisees."[68] This interpretation was fanned by the development of liberation theology and the rise of guerrilla-priests in Latin America.

The moral tone of the Movement attracted a number of religious individuals to the struggle. In my own Mormon parish in San Antonio, a number of the members joined La Raza Unida Party and a number of the other community organizations active at the time. The Movement to me, and many others like me, represented a variation of the social gospel. We were to work for the poor, to preach higher moral and political values, and to empower communities to challenge an evil society. Attending political masses, working with priests and lay leaders to empower poor parishioners, and placing the Movement within the context of a moral crusade served to radicalize religious life for many of us. We then interpreted many of our religious leaders' actions within a historical context of resistance against Anglo-American racism or paternalism.

The Church—as a religious entity—did not change drastically, notwithstanding many challenges to its ministries. But many Chicano followers did change. They saw the Church as having a role beyond the four walls of the chapel or the cathedral. They saw the gospel going beyond personal values to providing a framework for a just society. The moral authority of the Church was to be used to teach against the evils of poverty, discrimination, and capitalism. For activists, the changing role of the faithful in the Church, an institution that had functioned for decades as the maintainer of culture, helped in the reinterpretation of the Chicano experience. Taking the collective cultural experience of the Church as a basis, Chicano activists not only provided historicity to their struggle but also gave it a moral impetus. The intellectual dichotomy between those who accepted religion and those who rejected it remained significant throughout the Movement period, but for those who remained faithful, the new interpretation made them more adamant about working for social justice. This added to the new view of an active and resisting community.

Chicanas proved to be another sector of the community deeply affected by the reinterpretation of history. If Mexican American males suffered the burden of stereotypes, then Mexican American women suffered a double burden. What could be expected of the mothers, wives, and daughters of those men who were ahistorical, passive, lazy, and *mañana*-oriented? Arthur Rubel, one of those social scientists that Romano had taken to task for stereotyping Mexican American males, wrote about the Chicana: "[They are] ideally submissive, unworldly, and chaste."[69] They were possessions to be guarded and protected from the outside world. William Madsen went further in denigrating Mexican American women: "The Latin woman plays the perfect counterpart to the Latin male. Where he is strong, she is weak. Where he is aggressive, she is submissive. While he is condescending toward her, she is respectful toward him. A woman is expected to always display those subdued qualities of womanhood that make a man feel the need to protect her."[70] Spousal abuse, continued Madsen, was seen as deserved and as proof of profound love.

Gloria Molina de Pick argued that Chicanas suffered from the depiction of being chaste and submissive as well as seductive and representing the "most provocative of sexual adventures."[71] This contradiction, wrote Adaljiza Sosa Riddell, served to free American society from any responsibility for the Chicanas' oppression, and it kept Chicanas "preoccupied" with their "shortcomings." This conflictive dichotomy blamed Chicanas "for not being good mothers, for not keeping the family together, for working instead of staying home, or conversely, for being too oriented to their family, for having too many children, for not working, for staying home."[72] Mexican American women simply could not win. Either seen as submissive and passive or as seductive and responsible for familial shortcomings, they were even less a rational entity than their husbands, fathers, or sons.

Initially, the Movement's interpretation of women centered on their relationships to the family. At the Chicano Youth Liberation Conference, Chicanas, anxious to be seen as part of a united front, voted to declare that they did not want to be "liberated."[73] But the Movement, notwithstanding the chauvinism of some of its leaders, could not help but challenge patriarchy through its liberation rhetoric and through the opportunity it gave women to become involved in protest activities. Women, through their clerical skills, their willingness to do tedious jobs well, and their ability to follow through on assignments, became the organizational backbone of the Movement.

When Movement activities began in the early 1960s, precursors were few. Although they tended to be predominantly male, there were a significant number of women. A few women were known Movement-wide, but many others were part of the rank and file, whose influence remained at the local and regional level.

These women, once in the Movement, began to argue for inclusion in the new interpretation. "When we talk equality," wrote Longeaux y Vásquez, "we better be talking about total equality."[74] But rather than wait for the men to dominate the process, they set out to do the interpretation. Chicano activists often saw the historical Mexican woman as self-sacrificing—as the *abuelita,* or the Adelita who followed the man during times of upheaval. The poet José Montoya wrote:

> When I remember the *campos* [fields]
> . . . I remember my *jefita's* [mother's]
> *palote* [rolling pin]
> (I swear, she never slept)
> *Es tarde mi hijito* [it's late my son],
> cover up
> . . . a maternal reply mingled with
> the hissing of the hot *planchas* [iron]
> . . . *y la jefita* slapping tortillas
> . . . *y en el fil* [in the field], pulling
> her *cien* [one hundred]
> *libras del algodón* [pounds of cotton]
> . . . that woman—she only complains
> in her sleep.[75]

Chicanas saw themselves as more than self-sacrificing spouses or mothers. Like the male activists, they saw themselves as having a strong historical legacy but a diverse one. They accepted the role of the self-sacrificing woman as a legitimate part of the Chicana experience but complemented it with that of the labor leader who fought for the rights of working people, of the *soldadera* who fought with guns and rifles for freedom, and of the ideologue who wrote and spoke against injustices. Women were to be found wherever there was struggle.[76]

Most Chicana activists felt a need to remain within the mainstream of the Movement. They saw the liberation of community as the first goal. They argued, at least initially, that Chicanas first became ideologically conscious of discrimination as Chicanas rather than as women. But within the Movement, they demanded the room to deal with issues that affected them as mothers and as women. And they also sought an influential role in defining the direction of the community's liberation. Many men responded to the women's concerns positively. Activist scholar Martha Cotera remembered that most of the male leaders in La Raza Unida Party tended to be supportive. "I don't really remember the men as obstacles," she would say years later.[77]

The women's dialogue, first among themselves and then publicly in publications such as *Regeneración, Encuentro Femenil,* and other Chicano journals of the time, sought to define a new place for Chicanas. The new Chicana would stand alongside her man as the *soldadera* of the Mexican Revolution did, but she expected the partnership to be equal. And the definition of liberation now had to include freedom from *machismo* and the full freedom to participate in all aspects of the Chicano community's decision making. The political agenda had to concern itself with child care, employment and training for women, and a redefinition of familial roles.[78] Chicano activists, faced with a need for dedicated workers and confronted with their own "ideologically progressive" rhetoric, found themselves forced to open the Movement to women. Although the opening oftentimes seemed scarcely a crack to many, the women took advantage of it and reinterpreted their historical role within the Chicano community. If the men had struggled and resisted conquest and discrimination, then Chicanas had done the same. Chicana scholars, artists, essayists, and poets made sure that those within and without the Movement did not forget.

Chicanas also began exploring the special burden that they carried as women. Declared the platform of La Raza Unida Party in Colorado: "For our women . . . there exists a triple exploitation, a triple degradation; they are exploited as women, as people of *La Raza,* and they suffer from the poverty that straitjackets all of *La Raza.* We feel that without the recognition . . . of their special form of oppression . . . our movement will suffer greatly."[79] Like their black counterparts, these Chicanas sought to expand beyond the ideological boundaries set for them by male activists and white feminists. Chicanas saw their struggle in terms of community and family, even as they fought for equality at the personal level. Unbridled by the males' concept of honor, which saw political defeat as humiliating, these women continued to push for an end to racism and for collective empowerment in the face of strong opposition. Once they reinterpreted the Chicana experience as positive and heroic, they found the historical impetus to continue their activism.

Scholarly works of high quality, with a few exceptions, would come after the decline of the Movement. Some of them would even contradict the romanticism of the Movement-inspired histories. But most continued to offer a new and positive interpretation of the Chicano experience. Chicano Movement historians, trained or otherwise, had engaged in a historical discourse to discredit stereotypes and to combat the crisis of identity that many Mexican Americans confronted. Their history often worked chronologically backward. Their premise was that Chicanos were a strong and courageous people who had survived conquest, colonization, and racial brutality. Working back from that premise meant interpreting the "facts" to support the thesis. This new view of history allowed Chicanos to become the evaluators and legitimizers of their history and provided them the opportunity to define their historical significance and importance. Historical reinterpretation would be one of the most significant products of the Chicano Movement.

CHAPTER THREE

Chicanismo:
An Affirmation of Race and Class

In his work on Chicano politics, Juan Gómez-Quiñones argues that Chicano militants never quite built a political ideology that incorporated a correct class analysis.[1] That is, Chicano organizations did not develop an explicit class constituency with a program that identified capitalism as the enemy and that sought to work outside U.S. institutions that were hostile to the working class. Most Chicano organizations, according to Gómez-Quiñones, were at best reformist in nature and at worst reactionary with capitalist tendencies. Gómez-Quiñones is right if we are to measure Chicano political ideology using a traditional or even neo-Marxist approach.[2] The fact is that no major Chicano Movement organization produced the necessary polemics and writings to fashion an ideology that was explicitly class based and that promoted a revolutionary break from American society. Most Chicano activist organizations sought an amalgamation of all classes and social groups within the community. They believed that their strength would be enhanced by a small, progressive middle class not yet removed from its working-class origins, as well as by a marginalized lumpen element hostile to Anglo-Americans.

Most Chicano intellectuals were initially cultural nationalists, whose ideas, at times, paralleled those of nationalists involved in anticolonialist struggles throughout the world. Although the Chicano condition did not allow for a similar armed struggle, it did provide the political climate for nationalist and anti-imperialist rhetoric that called for interclass unity and a confrontation with Anglo-American racism through protest marches, ethnocentric rhetoric, electoral politics, and, for some, sabotage. There were those areas in Aztlán where Mexican Americans felt culturally, socially, and physically besieged. In some areas, police enforcement approximated brutality; in others, school children were segregated and emotionally abused; and in still others, vicious stereotypes were common. In these localities, Chicano activists were extremely hostile to American society, and they became more radical.

The Chicano militant rhetoric never truly became a nationalist critique on the question of a Chicano homeland, but it did provide a sense of consciousness as to Chicanos' status in American society. By consciousness, I mean an acute awareness rather than a profound understanding. This consciousness underscored the reality that Mexican Americans were for the most part working class. And they remained outside the American mainstream because there was no convergence between their working-class experience and the capitalist history of the United States. In that sense, Chicano activists were quite conscious of their class status. Although their sense of cultural nationalism led them to seek an amalgamation of all classes and social groups within the community, they never lost sight of the fact that most Chicanos were working class or poor.[3]

The Chicano Movement gained its strength from the working-class sector of the community and revealed its radicalism—not necessarily its militancy—within this sector. The constant preoccupation with racial origins and class position provided a cohesion to the struggle. Much of the polemics of the Movement centered on racial and class differences with the mainstream, and notwithstanding the large number of students, most of the Movement organizations' members were community-based, working-class adults and youths.[4] Race and class were two aspects of the Chicano experience that interested Chicano activists and intellectuals. In dealing with race and class in a historical sense, activists emulated the efforts of other nationalist movements in their "passionate search for a national culture." In speaking of this intellectual search that often led activists to romanticize the precolonial days, Franz Fanon, the black nationalist from Algeria who inspired a generation of cultural nationalists, remarked, "Because they realize they are in danger of losing their lives and . . . becoming lost to their people, these men [and women] relentlessly determine to renew contact once more with the oldest and most precolonial springs of life of their people."[5]

This nostalgia led Chicano activists to precolonial Mexico's indigenous civilizations, where they found great cities, brave warriors, and much knowl-

edge.[6] The Aztecs and the Mayas became central to the beginning of the
Chicano genealogy. This was not an original idea; many Mexican intellectuals during and shortly after the Mexican Revolution had written often and
ably about this part of the Mexican character. Other Mexican essayists in
the postrevolutionary period had done the same. But with time, many Mexican writers came to blame Mexican fatalism, alcoholism, *machismo,* and
criminality on the *indio* part of the Mexican character. The surge toward
capitalism had reduced earlier nationalist and Marxist discussions of the
Mexican working class to a discussion of social deficiency among the poorer
classes. But Chicano activists, still searching for their nationalist roots, continued to view their *mestizaje* (mixed bloodlines) in a revolutionary light.
The "Indian half" represented nobility, civilization, and courage. It had been
the barbarism of the Spaniard and later that of the landed class that had destroyed and subjugated the progress of the Mexican native.

The 1960s and 1970s produced a number of books that extolled the
Hispanic or Spanish roots of the Chicano and the "civilization" of the Spanish presence in the New World, with its universities, presses, newspapers,
cities, and such, but they did not come from Chicano scholars or intellectuals involved in the Movement. Most of this Hispanization came from those
with an integrationist view of American society. These were people who
sought to prove that Mexican Americans were as "civilized" and as democratic as the Anglo-American. They belonged to a generation for whom
scholars like Carlos Castañeda, Julian Samora, and Arthur L. Campa
spoke.[7] They highlighted the similarities between Anglo-American democratic and modern principles and those of the great men of Mexico and
Spain. Mexicans, like Americans, wrote Castañeda, were Christian, democratic, and moral.[8] This scholarship ran counter to what Chicano activists
promoted. Similarities to the dominant culture were not something to be exhibited. Those who sought them would continue to publish and speak, but
during the height of the Chicano Movement they were influential only in
certain areas where the Movement remained weak.

Chicano scholars, activists, and poets argued that *indigenismo* (the native character) permeated major aspects of Mexican American life. "Hardly
a barrio exists that does not have someone who is nicknamed 'el indio,'"
wrote Octavio Romano in 1974.[9] "Indian themes consistently have been
common subject matter for neighborhood . . . artists . . . and Aztec legends

still . . . tell and retell their stories in barrio living rooms . . . and Chicano newspapers."[10] Chicano activists and scholars found within their indigenous half that sense of difference that they sought to strengthen and expand in the consciousness of the average Mexican American. By stressing their *mestizaje,* they were in fact stressing their link to a more natural period when European influence and dominance were missing. For the Chicano activist, the pre-Columbian people represented the real birth of the Chicano nation. Chicanos chose to view the *indio* at the height of his or her power and culture. They bypassed the remnants, which had all but succumbed to the conquest and which were the subject of writers like Octavio Paz and Samuel Ramos, who wrote about the negative characteristics of the Mexican.[11]

In those Native American civilizations were the traces of a people who had mastered astronomy, mathematics, some forms of surgery, and agricultural production. These people also had a spiritual connection to the land. This royal heritage was important in the myth-making process. The Aztecs and Mayas had resisted conquest and domination, and although they were defeated their presence as a people did not totally die. This indigenous half of Mexico had risen with the Mexican Revolution of 1910 and still exhibited its resistance in the takeover of lands and in the indigenous organizations active during the 1960s.[12]

Indigenismo represented a part of the new heritage that Chicanos were trying to develop. "I am the eagle and serpent of Aztec civilization," declared "Corky" Gonzales in 1969.[13] Although Chicanos would never quite be successful in building lasting alliances with the American Indian Movement, they nevertheless saw that group's struggle as part of theirs. Chicanos were, for the most part, *mestizos,* and in order to find themselves they had to come to terms with that. This search for the Indian past led many to study Mexican history. They soon found that much of the work on Mexico's Indians, written by Anglo-American scholars, depicted the Aztecs and Mayas as bloodthirsty, warlike, and repressive of their people.[14] Many Chicanos began to look elsewhere for information. They read books by Mexican scholars and sought original manuscripts by Mexican Indians.[15] Some simply reconstructed writings by mainstream authors, gleaning every bit of information that contradicted the authors themselves. This search often led to the creation of a mythical past, in which Native Americans were "devoid of aggression, warfare . . . perfidy, treason, intoxication, [and] adultery."[16] The search for this past also took them to José Vasconcelos' ideas on the *raza cósmica.*[17] This concept of a new race of mixed blood and origin, which would overshadow other races intellectually and spiritually, captivated Chicano activists. To them, Chicanos were the *raza cósmica.*

What was most important about this concept of the *raza cósmica* was that it set Chicanos apart racially. Although Mexican Americans were accepted as Caucasians, by the late 1960s many Mexican American activists and others wanted to have their own category. As a senior in high school in 1969, I remember my friends and I adding "brown" as a racial category on job, scholarship, and financial-aid application forms. To be a "brown" meant we were different. Being different opened us to a new definition of our identity. This as-yet-undefined new category gave us an opportunity to engage in a "painful self-evaluation, a wondering search for [our] people, and most of all for [our] identity."[18] As young Chicanos, we were caught between two cultures, American and Mexican. *Chicanismo* was a blending of the two and was simultaneously an acceptance of both and a rejection of both. Most important, our *mestizaje* was our ticket out of white America.

It is important to understand that being different racially, or at least ethnically, meshed with the rejection of the liberal agenda and the reinterpretation of the past. It meant that Chicanos would not be measured by the same scale of success as would Anglo-Americans and other groups. By not accepting the rules, and by identifying themselves as historically and racially different, Chicanos could forge a new image. This new image was a first step toward recognition of their peoplehood. Chicanos accepted that they were not white, but more important, they accepted that they did not want to be white. For Chicano activists, the desire of previous generations of Mexican Americans to be "American" simply disguised a desire to assimilate into Anglo-American society. They believed that when Mexican Americans recognized and extolled their *indigenismo,* they would no longer seek to be "American."

The Chicano Movement activists and scholars, although promoting a new, indigenous Chicano, did so within the context of the Mexican American community's class experience. Carlos Muñoz placed the Chicano Student Movement within the context of a working-class experience. What he says about the student aspect of the Movement also applies to it as a whole:

"The Chicano [Student] Movement reflected . . . characteristics related to the . . . racial and class oppression experienced by the Mexican American working class. With rare exception, its leadership and rank and file came from that class. . . . Chicano youth radicalism represented a return to the humanistic cultural values of the Mexican working class. This . . . led to the shaping of a nationalist ideology, which . . . stressed the nonwhite indigenous aspects of Mexican working class culture."[19] The Chicano experience, according to activists, could not be seen as anything other than a working-class experience. And its leaders could not be anything other than working class.[20]

The leadership of the Mexican American middle class had lost the helm of the civil-rights movement in the barrio when it attempted to hold on to a middle-class liberal agenda. By the late 1960s, few of them had new ideas. Their abhorrence of the cultural nationalist rhetoric and their integrationist politics kept them from moving fully into the arena of confrontational politics.[21] They were seen as bankrupt of ideas by a new generation of activists who were influenced by the concepts being tossed around from California to Texas. The middle-class leaders were overly conscious of status. In areas like San Antonio, Tucson, Los Angeles, and Albuquerque, these middle-class Mexican Americans had developed their enclaves where they lived and shopped. This should not imply that they did not mingle with working-class Chicanos, for they did. But they always felt secure in their neighborhoods and in their professional or skilled circles. Although a number of them worked for their community, they did so with the understanding that they provided the leadership and that reforms would be instituted and arrived at in the manner by which they had obtained their middle-class status. Americanism, something still foreign to many in the barrio, was the only way up. Any deviation presented a potential threat. Leftism, except for some forms of liberal leftism, was not an option, and neither was a militant nationalism.

The Chicano Movement rejected this middle-class ethos and saw it as an ideology of collaboration or accommodation. This collaboration came in the form of political alliances, an affinity for American culture and tradition, and the loss of the Spanish language. Chicano activists could not understand why those in the middle class did not join the Chicano Movement organizations en masse, or why they chose to listen to American music, or why many in the middle class were losing their fluency in Spanish.[22] Most Chicano activists tended to judge the older generation and its admirers within cultural and economic parameters. All that most Chicano activists could see was the economic status of the Mexican American middle class, which took many of its members from the barrio. Their education, their Anglicized children, and their obsessive patriotism were all signs that they had traded in their Mexicanness. This was not true of all of them, but enough fit the mold in the eyes of activists to confirm the accusations.[23] "I look at myself," declared the poem *Yo Soy Joaquín,* "and see part of me that rejects my father and my mother and dissolves into the melting pot."[24]

In rejecting the middle class, Chicano activists tried to change the rules of the status game. The goal no longer was leaving the barrio for a home in the suburbs. Transforming the barrio's image became an important goal of the Movement. There were still drugs, gangs, and decaying neighborhood blocks, but the barrio also had homes, *tienditas, restaurantes,* churches, and a number of other symbols that to a Chicano meant survival and a vibrant life. Unlike the sterile images of white neighborhoods that Chicanos painted, the barrios had children playing, the smell of *tortillas* from the local *molino,* the smell of recently made bread from the *panaderías,* and the voices of street vendors selling their inexpensive products. The barrios even had names that seemed to identify something greater than just a geographical area: Barrio Libertad, La Esperanza, Benito Juárez, Cuauhtémoc, and so on. There was always the home of the respected family where members of the neighborhood congregated in times of tragedy or celebration. It is likely that some of these elements were already gone from many of the barrios by the 1960s, but to activists who set out to reject the American mainstream, these barrios did exist. And they existed everywhere.[25]

The barrios represented a mass of people waiting to be organized by the right kind of leadership. Most activists knew that barrio residents could not be organized if they were made to feel inferior or less than successful or acceptable. Although many Mexican American reformers had made sincere efforts to better the barrios in the past, they had often perceived the barrios as places to be changed. They enjoyed the culture, but they often found some of the traditions archaic and based on superstition. When they were unsuccessful in getting the barrio residents to do something they felt needed to be done, they placed most of the blame on them. Comments like "*no se le quita lo mexicano* (you can't take the Mexican out of them)," "Mexican standard time," and others revealed the impatience that some middle-class reformers felt toward their people.[26] Reforming the Mexican part of the soul seemed a top priority among reformers from the middle class. Chicano nationalists, on the other hand, saw the barrio as a place to preserve. Barrio Chicanos had survived American society by staying together in their enclaves, and the Chicano Movement sought to enhance, not change, the barrio. The barrios were the place where the Chicano working class lived and socialized, and where they could be organized into a potent political force. Chicano activists changed the approach of the middle-class reformers, who often lectured, chastised, or tried to lead by example.[27]

The clearest difference between the middle-class reformers and Chicano activists was their views of the barrio residents. The middle-class reformers saw most barrio residents as people whose limited education and humble economic circumstances placed them in a subordinate position. Barrio residents confronted an alien society that did not respect cultural traditions and that functioned by different rules. With few English-language skills and limited vocational or educational training, these residents were condemned to live in poor barrios in dilapidated housing and to perpetuate the same existence for their children. Their desire to maintain their language and traditions and their hesitation to chase after the American dream seemed only to confirm to these reformers the need to Americanize the barrio residents' way of thinking.[28]

Chicano activists, in contrast, saw no inherent weakness in the barrio residents, though they would have agreed with the reformers that there were problems in the barrio. Instead of perceiving barrio residents as semi-illiterate, weak, and without ambition, however, they often saw them as strong individuals who had survived racism and discrimination. Their wrinkled faces, sunburned features, and rough hands were not an indication of limited mobility but rather a confirmation of their work ethic and drive to get ahead. Their reluctance to move away from the barrio had nothing to do with provincialism or a desire to segregate. It had to do with the realization that Anglo-American society was not as attractive as some had thought. "I have come a long way to nowhere," decried Gonzales, "unwillingly dragged by that monstrous, technical, industrial giant called progress and Anglo society."[29] Abandoning the barrio to choose the American dream was to engage in a "pathetic" search for false happiness. *"Ser Chicano es vivir como humano* (to be a Chicano is to live like a human)," declared the *pinto* (jailbird) poet Ricardo Sanchez.[30] It also indicated a willingness to maintain community and preserve the culture. Students did not drop out of schools because they lacked parental support. Most Mexican American parents, Chicano activists argued, wanted their sons and daughters in school, but the schools were pushing them out. Other parents were simply too poor to keep their children in school. For Chicano activists, the residents of the barrios did not need to be Americanized to take control of their lives. What they needed was a sense of empowerment and the knowledge of how to acquire power. Said Raul Ruiz, a La Raza Unida Party candidate from California, "The tragedy is not that our people suffer so much in this society, but rather that they cannot effectively interpret that oppression."[31] In the view of activists, most Chicanos in the barrio were to be commended for what they had accomplished in their lives, considering the daily obstacles they faced. Mexican Americans needed to learn not only to resist but to overcome their oppression. Chicano nationalists rejected Marxist notions of the Chicano experience, which saw Mexican Americans only as a mass of exploited workers.

Kingsville, Texas, where I became deeply involved in the Movement, is a good place to study the role that the barrio residents played in the mind of the Chicano activist. It must be pointed out that Kingsville was not representative of all Chicano communities in the Southwest. It had unique characteristics, such as being a community with a naval base, a four-year university, and the world-famous King Ranch. Also, the experience of Chicanos in South Texas had its unique aspects.[32] Still, there are things about the Movement that can be learned by looking at a community such as Kingsville. After all, much of the initial organizing in Chicano communities throughout the Southwest sought to duplicate activities by other Chicanos that had proved successful. The takeover of Crystal City, Texas, became a model for many communities, just as it did for this particular one.

Kingsville in the early 1970s was about 50 percent Mexican American. Many of them worked for the nearby naval base, the chemical plant, the university, or the King Ranch, which sat on the outskirts of town. Much of the rest of the Mexican American population worked in the school district or the small-service industry, or commuted to nearby Corpus Christi. A small number of bureaucrats and teachers from the university, lawyers, pharmacists, and social workers made up the Kingsville Mexican American middle class. Politically, they vacillated between accommodation and confrontation with the conservative Anglo-American population. Movement activities at Texas A & I University began as early as 1965. Between 1965 and 1975, students, faculty, and individuals in the community engaged in a number of Movement activities. They participated in major state and national movement activities, led walkouts in the public schools, forced the establishment of an ethnic studies center, and established an underground newspaper.[33]

Leadership of the movement in Kingsville eventually transferred to Raul Villarreal, a college dropout who worked as a bartender throughout the four years I attended school there. In the early 1970s, Villarreal and Jorge Guerra, another student and a former army officer, helped found the Trabajadores Unidos de Kingsville. This workers' association brought together Chicanos from the chemical plant and the school district, though the majority of its members came from the maintenance department of the university. The Trabajadores Unidos also included students and several professionals, but from the beginning only members of the working class could become officers of the predominantly male organization.

Our job as college students centered on being the support staff for the organization.[34] We reserved the university classrooms for meetings, typed out agendas, notified members of the meetings, took minutes, and performed the necessary clerical work to keep the organization functioning. Villarreal and members of the Trabajadores Unidos also helped organize a community advisory board for the local Texas Rural Legal Aid office in Kingsville. Here again, most of the officers and rank-and-file members were working-class residents. Middle-class professionals, who had in the past populated and dominated such committees in the barrio, were explicitly excluded from most of the board's functions.[35] Although the working-class members depended on us for information and "guidance," the decision making was by majority vote. It should be pointed out that the Kingsville activists were particularly astute at identifying the issues of major concern in that community. Consequently, there were few divisive debates on the direction to take.

When La Raza Unida Club, a Chicano organization at Texas A & I, sponsored activities, they were directed toward the working-class community. They were usually cosponsored by the Trabajadores Unidos or another community group. The club would reserve a small park that belonged to the university, provide food—with money from the Student Union Governing Board, which it controlled through student elections—and hire local musicians to entertain. No activity would end, however, without a pitch for La Raza Unida Party and the Movement in general. It also became common for us to honor community organizers who had been active throughout their lives. They were a symbol of the historical continuity in our struggle.

As members of the Raza Unida Club, we received constant indoctrination on the role of the working class, or *la gente,* in the Movement.[36] All-day training sessions were held in a three-bedroom house across the street from the university. There, seated in old folding chairs, we listened to Villarreal expound on the virtues of La Raza. He quoted Vasconcelos, sprinkled with a little Che Guevara, Fidel Castro, José Angel Gutiérrez, and "Corky" Gonzales, and then usually put it all into context by providing an analogy that one of the old Chicanos in the barrio had shared with him.[37] In places like Kingsville there were no major heroes, only the collective personification of the working-class *mexicano.* David Torres and Melissa Amado, in their work on Mexican Americans in Tucson, argue that "Mexican-based culture has consistently recognized the primacy of el pueblo, over individual rights and freedoms. While the collectivist ideology is philosophically based on Catholicism, and perhaps even on ancient cultures that preceded the invasion by the Spaniards, it has been buttressed by historical praxis. The masses have consistently had to bond together in their struggles against one or another set of elites."[38] This sense of collectivism was what Chicano activists saw as the key element in the barrio's heroism. Its ability to rally around itself during times of trouble had maintained the vibrancy of the culture in some areas. When La Raza had been divided culturally (through assimilation), politically, or geographically, it usually had lost its battles.[39] A return to this collectivism at a time when mainstream society demanded individualism and the pursuit of the economic pie became the Chicano activists' goals.

As student activists, we were to follow strict rules in dealing with the community. We were never to get drunk or use profanities at any community function. We were also not to try to dominate any meeting or gathering.

Our approach was one of respect. The *viejitos* and *viejitas* represented warriors of another era. Although our approach in Kingsville may have been slightly overdone, it was an approach emulated by other activists in different areas.

When we confronted middle-class Chicanos of the university, we often chided them for moving away from the *comunidad*. With time, many of them were forced to use the rhetoric that emphasized the legitimizing role of the community. *La gente* represented the vanguard of the Movimiento. They provided the stimulus to all that we as students or professionals did. Our role as activists was not to lead or even to push too hard but rather to march along, learn, facilitate, and teach the skills the community needed. *La gente,* when empowered, had the progressive instincts to solve many of its problems. To Villarreal, the answer to most of the issues came from philosophical discussions with the people from the barrio. This did not imply that Villarreal and the rest of us were not constantly trying to move Kingsville's Chicanos toward achieving particular goals. We were. And by the mere nature of our intensity and hard work, we often led, but we did so with a minimum of titles or positions. Villarreal, and consequently the rest of us, saw it as imperative to stay within the mainstream of the Chicano working class. That is, we pushed only as hard as the community people were willing to accept. This explains, for example, our conservative agenda when it came to familial matters, our militant politics notwithstanding.

The Kingsville experiment was in reality an effort to duplicate the tactics used in the successful political takeover of Crystal City, Texas, in 1970. There, José Angel Gutiérrez had developed a grassroots organization named Ciudadanos Unidos and had taken advantage of a student protest to galvanize support for an electoral revolt. He had worked for months before the school walkout to rebuild Chicano morale, which had been badly shaken by the unraveling of the 1963 revolt mentioned previously in chapter 1. Gutiérrez's task had been to convince Chicanos that not only could they succeed politically against the Anglo-American but that they could also govern themselves. For working-class individuals unused to directing, presiding, or governing, that became a major challenge. In building the organization, Gutiérrez initially moved away from assuming any public leadership role. He did not want to intimidate those who saw his academic credentials as major achievements or alienate those who mistrusted middle-class reformers. A point should be made at this juncture. This type of nonelitist organizing would eventually give way to various forms of *personalismo* (charismatic leadership) and power struggles. These struggles eventually became one of the primary reasons for the demise of the Movement. But serious attempts at participatory-type democracy would remain as the eventual goals for most Chicano organizations, and this would distinguish them from the more-hierarchical Hispanic organizations that succeeded them.

At first, Ciudadanos Unidos of Crystal City admitted only men, but quickly it became an organization for the whole family. The change did not come about because of male benevolence or the need for a patriarchal structure. Rather, the women took it upon themselves to change the situation. Shortly after the first victories in 1970, women stormed the dance hall where the organization met. Led by Luz Gutiérrez, the women demanded to be included in the decision making. Many of the men did not like the idea of their wives being in a dance hall with other men, but the women remained firm in their demand and won out.[40] The women's confidence in taking a strong negotiating stand grew out of their mass participation in the activities of La Raza Unida Party. Also, the women of Crystal City had a core group of women leaders who were well educated or had years of experience as organizers. These were women such as Luz Gutiérrez, who became the party's first county chairperson; Virginia Músquiz, a longtime activist often referred to as Gutiérrez's mentor; Viviana Santiago, who went on to become a lawyer and was a close adviser to Gutiérrez; and Severita Lara, one of the student leaders of the school walkouts that led to the founding of La Raza Unida Party. Within a short period, the women of Crystal City made up much of the elected leadership of the organization and also held many of the elected positions in the county and city.[41]

Ciudadanos Unidos, especially as led by the women, sponsored family activities and engaged in service projects to benefit the community. The organization practiced a grassroots democracy that provided many working-class individuals the opportunity to participate and vote. The process became so much a part of the political life of Crystal City that the eventual challenge to Gutiérrez and La Raza Unida Party came from those dissatisfied not by the process but by the decisions made. Gutiérrez, often seen as a *caudillo* by those outside Crystal City and by his rivals in the Movement, did not always have the votes to have things his way. There were times when he was excluded from some of the more important committees within Ciudadanos Unidos, and he barely hung onto the leadership of the party in Crystal City.[42]

Organizations such as Trabajadores Unidos de Kingsville and Ciudadanos Unidos differed significantly from middle-class organizations such as LULAC, the American G.I. Forum, and PASSO, which were hierarchical, dependent on a core of highly educated middle-class men for direction, and susceptible to influence from outside the Mexican American community. By the 1970s, these middle-class organizations had lost their mass-action strategies and depended heavily on small paid staffs to run their day-to-day activities. They had also become dependent on government funds to promote their agendas. Chicano Movement groups, on the contrary, lived or died—and many of them died—on their ability to rally their working-class members to collective action.

This preoccupation with the working class was not limited to Texas. Salomón Baldenegro, Lupita Castillo, Cecilia Baldenegro, Raul Grijalva, and others who headed the Movement in Tucson, Arizona, were all products of working-class families, and promoted a working-class slant to the Movement.[43] They were first-generation Americans, which meant that most of their parents had not yet gone through a complete process of acculturation. They grew up in homes where Spanish was spoken, histories of Mexico were narrated, and the American system had not been fully accepted.[44] As poor working-class youth they also "grew up in an environment where people who exploited [them] were middle class."[45] For many Chicano activists like the Tucson group, their experience with Mexican Americans in the middle class—teachers, small businessmen, policemen— proved to be quite negative. Many of these middle-class, integrated Mexican Americans were in essence the enforcers of Anglo-American culture. As policemen they tended to arrest more Chicanos, as teachers they punished or failed Chicano students more often, and as employers they gave their Chicano employees less opportunity for advancement. Most of the middle-class Chicanos sought tenaciously to be seen as different from the working-class Chicanos. Unlike the prewar era, when most Mexican Americans sought a sense of community to survive Anglo-American prejudices, in the late

1950s and early 1960s many middle-class Mexican Americans had become philosophically and economically distant from the status-immobile working class.[46]

Working-class Chicanos in Tucson, a southwestern city with a sizable Mexican American middle class, found it difficult to find alliances outside their class. Instead, they found their world within the barrio. They grew up speaking Spanish, with relatives living nearby, and in proximity to the border. When Baldenegro and others became part of the Movement, they found that many of the working-class Chicanos approved of their activities, as compared with middle-class Mexican Americans, who saw their status compromised by this activism.[47] The men and women involved in Movement activities in Tucson shared many of the characteristics of other Chicano activists. They grew up among strongly nationalistic, working-class parents, and they experienced racism at an early age. This background led them to reject those who stood outside the mainstream of the barrio. Said Baldenegro, "There were two kinds of Chicanos in the Movement, the discoverers and the enforcers. The discoverers were those who rediscovered their roots . . . born-again Chicanos. The enforcers were those of us who knew who we were. We knew our culture was good."[48] The enforcers had grown up resisting the no-Spanish-speaking rule in schools, being cynical of blind patriotism, and never accepting the stereotypes they constantly heard in school, in the media, and on the streets. While many youth of the 1960s were facing an identity crisis, young people like Salomón, Lupita, and Cecilia were looking for a reinforcement of their culture.

In accepting the working-class nature of the Mexican American community, activists emphasized the cultural traditions of the working class. Music became an important part of the Movement. José Reyna, in referring to Tejano music, wrote: "Chicanos, not having a nation in the political sense, which would then provide access to all the other institutions, have had to forge a culture in an auspicious way to say the least. Chicano music in Texas has certainly developed in this manner to a great extent. That is, it emerged and developed as an integral—and distinctive—part of Chicano culture."[49]

Manuel Peña, a cultural anthropologist, posited that the development of *conjunto* music from a folk-type musical novelty to a full-fledged and popular musical alternative to *orquesta* or *mariachi* music came in response to intraethnic conflict among Chicanos and to a cultural assault by English music. Wrote Peña: "Conjunto music's . . . rapid movement toward a common stylistic expression and its . . . entrenchment in the Texas-Mexican working class consciousness . . . is tied . . . to (1) that group's response to the challenge posed against traditional Mexican culture by a growing and increasing influential class of upwardly mobile people who espoused the American ideology of assimilation; and (2) the former's . . . recognition not only of its ethnic isolation, but its existence as an *economic class* 'for itself'" (author's italics).[50] Peña goes on to explain that *conjunto* music became the banner of the Chicano working class in its fight to keep the barrio from the *agringados* (those who have become acculturated or assimilated, or who emulate Anglo-Americans). According to Peña, the music became *la música de la gente pobre* (poor people's music).[51] This music had been around since the early twentieth century but became more pervasive with the growth of radio among Mexican Americans. Unfortunately, there have been no studies of the radio as a community institution among Mexican Americans, with the exception of a few lines by Reyna in his "Tejano Music as an Expression of Cultural Nationalism."[52]

For Reyna, the musicians promoted some aspects of the Chicano Movement's cultural renaissance. But it is important to differentiate the musicians of whom Reyna speaks with those mentioned in Peña's work. Peña's musicians were older, usually self-taught, and most often from the rural areas where they followed musical traditions. These musicians often spoke little English, and there were few elements of American influence in their compositions. On the contrary, the Chicano musicians about whom Reyna writes had bands with names like La Raza de Houston, Latin Breed, La Herencia, The Mexican Revolution, La Patria, La Onda Chicana, La Conexión Mexicana, and Tortilla Factory. These were musicians who had been influenced greatly by American styles, and most were educated musically in high school marching or stage bands. They used a number of the instruments of the older *orquesta* and, at times, added the accordion. These groups tended to play a greater variety of music than the *conjuntos*, including songs in English. They played to younger and more urban audiences. They were also more likely to call themselves Chicanos and to be part of the music that was referred to as *la onda chicana*. The father of this music was undoubtedly Little Joe and his group La Familia.[53] One of his songs,

"Las Nubes," was considered the Chicano national anthem, even though it had nothing to do with politics or ideology–in fact, few of the Chicano songs did.

For Chicano activists, Chicano or *conjunto* music served a political purpose. Wrote Reyna, "It is obvious that they [Chicano musicians] are promoting Chicanismo and their involvement in the Movement goes beyond the mere names."[54] Reyna served as the director of the ethnic studies program at Texas A & I University in Kingsville. While he was there, his program sponsored numerous concerts by Chicano bands and used them to gain the support of the students and members of the community for converting the ethnic studies program into a Chicano studies center. He also used the music to socialize Chicanos into the Movement. I remember that one of the requirements for students in his ethnic studies course was to meet at the local bar managed by Raul Villarreal and sing Mexican and Chicano revolutionary songs. After hours of singing songs about *revolución* and Chicano pride, most of us left feeling proud of who we were and anxious to engage in Movimiento activities.

Chicano resistance songs were not as numerous or as varied as those of many nationalist movements elsewhere. There were songs from the farmworker struggle and some about *carnalismo* (brotherhood) or the Movement, but not as many as might have been expected. Chicano activists simply coopted much of the music already written and sung by Mexican and Chicano musicians. One of the favorite themes of songs in the Chicano repertoire became the Mexican Revolution of 1910. The songs' messages of struggle, their praise of men and women who had fought for the poor and the land, and their often melancholic stories and tragic endings seemed appropriate mood-setters for Chicanos who believed themselves to be in a struggle. Of all the wars and resistance movements Mexican history offered, the one with which Chicanos could identify most was with this revolt of poor peasants and Indians against the upper class and foreigners. For Chicanos in the Movement, this reinterpreted history once again represented the Anglo-American as foreign and middle-class Mexican Americans as collaborators. To struggle against them meant to continue the revolution.[55] Being part of the most significant event in Mexican history provided Chicanos a historical legitimacy that no American experience could provide.

Chicano activism keenly reflected the community's working-class nature, notwithstanding middle-class activism or the influence of the student sector. All of the major organizations that recruited Chicanos and indoctrinated them with the politics of Aztlán were composed predominantly of working-class individuals, and much of the symbolism used by these organizations emerged from their class status. Most of these groups extolled their indigenous past, agitated on behalf of the poorest sector of the barrios and *pueblos,* sought some form of distribution of wealth, and for the most part collaborated only with those in the middle class who accepted the aforementioned premises. There were to be a number of groups under the guise of the Movement who still followed the precepts of the liberal agenda. But although some of them were successful in their efforts, they never quite had the ideological or cultural impact of the organizations that retained their class consciousness.[56]

The development of the working-class orientation shifted the politics of status and assimilation to one of cultural identity and empowerment.[57] Assimilation and attainment of middle-class individuality gave way to the search for solutions to the problems in the barrio. Those who had never sought assimilation but who had seen Mexico fade as a cultural and intellectual center for Chicanos now saw a new value in organic *chicanismo.* No more did Chicanos have to look south or north for that stimulus but only within their barrio to find their values as a people. Race and class, once a means by which Chicanos were ridiculed or discriminated against, now became symbols of the unique character of La Raza.

CHAPTER FOUR

Strategies for Aztlán:
Creating a Cultural Polity

The rejection of the liberal agenda, the reinterpretation of the Chicano experience, and the affirmation of the racial and class status of Chicanos all had political implications. But because the Movement remained regionally focused and had very identifiable regional leaders and groups, it never quite had the homogeneity Chicano activists wanted. Rather than one or two unifying individuals and organizations, the Chicano Movement was a collective of heterogeneous community and campus activists. No one person or group dominated the Movement. This prevented activists from agreeing on which change should come first or even what the approach to the struggle should be. The varying degrees of urgency they felt toward the different problems produced different goals and plans. Geography and demography also affected the political orientation and strategies of the activists. Those like Gutiérrez, who lived in areas with Mexican American majorities, saw the Movement as a vehicle for political control. Those who lived in areas where Chicanos were a small minority saw their role as one of politically educating the Chicano masses or promoting Chicano culture. The urban activists saw the need for alliances with other "oppressed" groups, whereas those in the rural areas were cultural purists who shunned power-sharing coalitions. Chicanos in the universities saw the United States as imperialistic and called for worldwide revolution. Barrio activists were more concerned with racial discrimination and cultural genocide and regarded participation in international struggles to be political deviancy.[1] There were those who transcended these political multidivisions, but without a national organization, or a widely disseminated publication, they were unable to create a greater organizational homogeneity within the

Movement.[2] What occurred was the development of numerous strategies, with major organizations becoming known for particular issues and smaller ones for overt action. The political activities were attempts at practical application of the rhetoric and the nationalist ideas of the Movement. Chicanos, once having defined the need for changes, had to respond with a political solution. In doing so, they sought to give practical meaning to terms such as Chicano power, Aztlán, liberation, *carnalismo,* justice, and self-determination. By themselves these terms were empty militant words. In the context of activities of the Chicano organizations, however, they represented a strategy for empowerment. The politics of the Movement were politics of reaction. Faced with overwhelming problems, the activists sought to create a rhetoric of liberation that would inspire their followers to gird up for the fight. Often this rhetoric became utopian or would be advanced in an ideological sphere that transcended practical realities. Yet Chicano activists continually attempted to find practical application for their rhetoric of liberation.

To better understand this last phase of the Chicano Movement, let us examine the political strategies and the rhetoric of three of the four major Movement organizations and those of several of the smaller groups active then. The UFW set the tone for much of the symbolism of the Movement. The Crusade for Justice provided the ideological premise. And La Raza Unida Party provided the model of what *chicanismo* could accomplish. The three organizations contributed much of the rhetoric and the ideas for the social catharsis that occurred in the barrios during the 1960s and 1970s. Though the organizations came into conflict with one another, they nonetheless provided much of the political rhetoric and the ideas of the Movement. These organizations, as well as others, promoted particular ideas or political morals, though not necessarily with the same priority. These ideas and morals, translated into political initiatives, served as the basis for Chicano political thought and strategy. Central to this thought and strategy was that Mexican Americans had been oppressed for too long and now were ready to mobilize with their own ideas, leaders, and organizations. Their Mexicanness or *chicanismo* would play a prominent role. Even among more leftist or Marxist Chicano groups, this identity became of paramount importance. In the Plan de Delano, the first document outlining the UFW's position, the farmworkers declared: "The Mexican race has sacrificed itself for the last hundred years. . . . Our sweat and our blood have fallen on [the] land to make other men rich. . . . We are sons of the Mexican Revolution, a revolution of the poor seeking bread and justice. . . . Wherever there are Mexican people . . . our movement is spreading like flames across a dry plain."[3]

Although many later charged that Chávez downplayed his ethnicity, it was his ethnicity that launched the UFW. His insight into the Mexican workers' character, their customs, their quiet outrage, their machismo, their family unity, and their sense of dignity gave him an advantage over others who had tried to organize them before.[4] His desire to remain close to the farmworkers and share the same hardship endeared him to his followers. To many, Chávez remained to the end another Mexican farmworker but one with radical ideas and the stamina to succeed where others had not.

Chávez knew how to use the symbolism familiar to the Mexican population. He chose the anniversary of Mexican independence, September 16, to launch his first *huelga* in 1965, and he used Benito Juárez's words, "*El respeto al derecho ajeno es la paz* (respect for individual rights creates peace)," in his Plan de Delano.[5] Although most farmworkers were only semiliterate, they nonetheless knew and could identify with Miguel Hidalgo and Benito Juárez.[6] The Mexican school system and the patriotic festivities had made sure of that. The union flag, which depicted a black eagle on a red background, resembled the Mexican flag. It provided an air of revolution and brought to mind a part of history, the Mexican Revolution, and its struggle between the "haves" and the "have nots." The most important symbol of the UFW, however, was the banner of the Virgin of Guadalupe. "We carry la Virgen de Guadalupe because she is ours, *all ours,* Patroness of the Mexican people," declared the Plan de Delano.[7] By bringing the church into the farmworker movement, even as others sought to distance themselves from it, Chávez identified himself as belonging within the mainstream of the Mexican and Mexican American communities. The symbol of the Virgen had played an important role in Mexico's independence, in the Cristero revolt (a Catholic uprising), and the Mexican Revolution of 1910. Few things were as ingrained in the Mexican mind as Catholicism and the Virgen de Guadalupe. Staying close to the church placed the farmworkers' movement within a conservative and legitimate boundary.[8] It made their militancy acceptable to many moderate and conservative Mexican Americans.

The Virgen also provided a moral force to the farmworker effort. Through the morality of its cause, the union believed it could win its struggle. Like Tijerina, Chávez wanted to stir the American public's compassion and sense of fair play. He also wanted to engage in a form of organizing that would not bring about a repressive reaction from the Anglo-American population. Chávez believed that the farmworkers were unlikely to engage in confrontational activities that they might well lose unless they felt their cause to be more than economic or political. The nonviolent approach, and the Virgin Mother, gave the union a moral high ground from which to attack its opposition. Unlike most of the other important organizations within the Movement, the UFW wanted the wide participation of all Americans in the struggle. Rather than divide the struggle into Chicano versus Anglo-American, or farmworkers versus capitalists, the farmworker leadership sought to make it a battle between good and evil, compassion and insensitivity, fairness and injustice. Most Americans, the leadership felt, would consider themselves compassionate and would tend to side with the poor farmworkers. Since many of the people would not consider themselves affected directly by the union contracts, they could side with the union without fearing it as they feared the AFL-CIO, the Teamsters, or other labor conglomerates.

In the periphery of the UFW organizing areas, many union members were sympathetic to the separatist or more militant aspects of the Movement, and they participated in some of the more radical activities of other organizations. But when it came to farmworker activities, they toed the UFW line. Since the Movement activists as a whole saw themselves as working for the poor of the barrio, the farmworkers' high moral attitude seemed attractive to many of them. Other organizations, more mainstream or liberal, admired the morality of the farmworkers' struggle.[9]

Because of their "moral high ground" approach, the union called its struggle a social movement rather than just an organizing campaign. The concept of a social movement revealed the union's desire to legitimize the role of the farmworker. The inability to successfully organize farmworkers in the past had often been blamed on the fact that this type of employment represented an archaic way to earn a living and seemed destined to fade as a livelihood. Many unions saw organizing them as an impossibility and chose to ignore this population, hoping it would cease to be a labor pool. Others had tried in the past—Ernesto Galarza was the last one in the late 1950s—but most had given up, finding the opposition too well organized and the farmworkers too incapable of being organized.[10] The UFW leadership quickly saw the necessity of doing more than just forming a union. They wanted farmwork to be a legitimate form of employment, and they wanted these, the least of the American workers, to gain from the fruit of their labor. Only by exciting the farmworkers with the idea of a social movement could they get the commitment, sacrifice, and valor they needed to establish a strong union. "Our union is not just another union. It is a movement," Chávez often repeated.[11]

This aspect of social Movimiento required, in the beginning at least, that the farmworkers' union remain independent of outside forces. To Chávez, the strength of the union could be measured by the ability and willingness of the membership to pay its dues and provide for the union's day-to-day expenses. He refused to follow the lead of black activist groups who received many of their funds from mainstream organizations or philanthropies.[12] Any group's willingness or unwillingness to pay its way revealed its capacity to stay afloat when difficult times came. The UFW was not adverse to fundraising or donations—after all, its support committees throughout the country provided much-needed resources. But the union leadership did not want to be indebted to any organization that could then seek to influence the UFW's policies. Also, Chávez and the rest of the leadership sought to place the sole responsibility of the union's survival on the farmworkers themselves.[13] Organizers were paid a meager amount to live on. And Chávez himself refused to better his own economic situation as long as the union remained limited in its victories. By not allowing external funding or salary levels to play a role in the union's decision making, the UFW felt itself independent and free to follow its own course of action.

This course of action was based on the wide participation of the American public and on a nonviolent attack on the growers. This nonviolent approach, while emulating the style of the Reverend Martin Luther King, went for its philosophical foundations to Mahatma Gandhi, who had constructed a massive social movement to free India from the British. In the early period, Chávez did not believe that King's approach of swaying people to action without an organizational structure would prove effective. Chávez believed in small house meetings and small group discussions as the manner in which to organize people to action. King's mass rallies did not often go beyond inspiring or exciting people around an unfocused action. Chávez's perception eventually changed, but in the early stages of the union's development he saw Malcolm X as someone who understood better the principles of organization. Said Chávez: "The approach that Malcolm X used was the house meeting—what we use—he was doing those things that we know pay: being patient and just accumulating, committing people and so forth. And he's gone, but the movement continues."[14]

Although articulated within the context of a union contract, Chávez's vision for the farmworkers went beyond collective bargaining. The UFW wanted respect for the Mexican field laborer to go along with the better wages, workers' insurance, sick leave, and vacation time. Rather than just make life tolerable for farmworker families until their children became educated and left the fields, the UFW wanted farmworkers to stand alongside Teamsters, plumbers, factory workers, and others who saw their livelihood as respectable.[15] In essence, Chávez wanted American society to accept the Mexican farmworker where he or she stood and to legitimize a skill that had become Mexicanized over time. Even though he accepted the presence of the Filipino workers in his union, Chávez understood that the ranks of the farmworker movement would be replenished by mostly Mexican workers. His search for legitimacy reflected the most profound acceptance of and desire to promote the working-class nature of the Chicano community. Chávez did not seek educational programs to "lift" laborers out of the fields, or welfare handouts to help the farmworker until he or she died. The farmworker—as a result of whose labor America ate vegetables and fruits and drank wine—had a place in society. The farm labor contract was one manifestation of that truth.[16] The farm labor contract, preceded by strikes, boycotts, and a wholesale promotion of the Mexican identity, served as the UFW's political strategy. Chávez's nonviolent approach also contributed to the politics of Aztlán.

Although Chávez became the target of some harsh criticism by more radical groups, his union and its followers would remain the most Mexicanized and most predominantly working-class organization of the Movement and its most important symbol. Its activities would be the subject of more art and music than any other Movimiento group. And the UFW would transcend the Movement to remain active long after most other activist organizations declined and disappeared. Its songs, flags, picket-line songs, and leader remained symbols of the Movement thirty years after its founding.

If the UFW's politics extolled and promoted the working-class nature of the Mexican community, the political strategy of the Crusade for Justice emphasized ideology derived from national origins and barrio culture. In his poem *Yo Soy Joaquín,* Gonzales wrote, "Mexicano, Español, Latin, Hispano, Chicano. I look the same. I feel the same. I cry and sing the same. I am the masses of my people and I refuse to be absorbed."[17]

The Crusade took the basic yearnings for respectability of the Mexican American middle class and radicalized them into an ethnocentric surge of racial pride. This pride required an identity independent and separate from that of the Anglo-American. In fact, separation and antagonism became an unspoken prerequisite to the attainment of this identity. In a speech to California students on February 22, 1968, Gonzales exhorted them to shun integration into Anglo-American society by abandoning mainstream institutions and politics. And he urged them to become involved in discovering their history and culture and teaching other Chicanos to be proud of who they were.[18]

Gonzales sought a national consciousness for Chicanos. He attempted to accomplish this with his political statements and his manifestos. During his participation with Tijerina in the Poor People's campaign, he became the chief author of a document released by the Chicano delegation. Titled, "We Demand: Statement of Chicanos of the Southwest in the Poor People's Campaign," the document called for the institutionalization of the Chicano community within the barrios of the Southwest through complete control of resources and public entities. Self-determination became operational through militant rhetoric.

> We demand that our schools be built in the same communal fashion as our neighborhoods. . . . We demand a . . . free education from kindergarten to college, . . . [that] Spanish be the first language, . . . [and that] textbooks be rewritten to emphasize . . . contributions of Mexican Americans. . . . We want our living areas to fit the needs of the family. . . . We demand that . . . the land be given back. . . . We demand seed money to organize . . . trade, labor, welfare, [and] housing . . . unions. . . . We demand . . . the creation of a neighborhood community court to deal with crime. . . . We demand that businesses serve our community.[19]

The demands went beyond any presented by civil-rights leaders and may have been one of the reasons for a rift between Chicano and African American leaders of the campaign. The integrationist approach of the black leaders was unacceptable to Gonzales, who quickly moved toward the conceptualization of a Chicano homeland.

On March 27–31, 1969, the Crusade for Justice sponsored the first Chicano Youth Liberation Conference in Denver, inviting thousands of young people from throughout the country to address the question, "Where do the barrio's youth, the student, the rural Chicano, the *campesino* fit into the Chicano Movement?"[20] Held at El Centro de la Crusada, the conference focused on two issues: social revolution and cultural identity. In the areas of social revolution, panel discussions were held on organizational techniques, politics and philosophies, self-defense against police aggression, and the planning of protests and demonstrations. The session on cultural identity centered on discussions of the roles of Chicano literature, Movimiento newspapers, and music. Gonzales had decided to hold the conference to provide cohesion to what seemed a movement whose parts did not add up to a whole. He also saw the need to connect the college students with the barrio youth. "Many youth who graduate from college leave the community and never come back," said Gonzales later. "We had to start breaking this down, so that the barrio *bato* had a relationship with the student." This relationship would have a mutual benefit. The college students were to provide philosophical and analytical depth to the barrio youth's rebelliousness, while becoming immersed in what Gonzales called the "mud . . . dirt . . . and blood of the urban experience of the barrio." It was a union of intellect and experience, skill and *corazón.*[21]

Attending the conference were representatives of all the major Chicano student groups in the country. There were the United Mexican American Students; the Mexican American Youth Association; the Third World Liberation Front from Berkeley; the Brown Berets, a paramilitary group with chapters throughout the Southwest; the Mexican American Student Organization from Arizona State University; the Young Lords, a Puerto Rican group from New York and Chicago; and numerous other smaller groups. Nearly 1,500 young people attended. They came anxious to find a national leadership and develop the presence that the Black Power Movement had achieved by that time.[22] They also came aroused by the turmoil of the times. This was the Nixon era; a time of strong student movements in the United

States, Europe, and Latin America; and the height of the Vietnam War. It might well be said that revolution was in the air. Because of this, wrote Gómez-Quiñones in his *Mexican Students por La Raza,* "[Mexican] students were predisposed to note the contrast of conditions in their community in comparison with the situation of the more privileged sectors of U.S. society. They became hypersensitive to the deplorable political, social and economic status of the Mexican community and the even starker realization that this was progressively worsening. . . . A need to develop an historical understanding of the Mexican experience became paramount."[23] When the students and youthful activists arrived, they were anxious to be molded into a movement at the national level. Up to that time, there were movement efforts in California, Texas, Arizona, and New Mexico, but no national movement.

Never before had so many Chicano youth come together to explore their identity and talk about change. The feelings were euphoric as the young people talked about conditions in their barrios, protests, organizing victories, major adversaries, and what the future might hold for the "new" Mexican American. They experienced an important bonding as they slept together at La Crusada building and were fed by people from Denver's Mexican American community. There were many natural leaders, chosen by their peers to lead the Movement in their locality, but none came to lead at the conference. Everyone soon realized that one individual, Gonzales, would take the spotlight at the conference. The gathering served as a platform from which he disseminated his views, which soon dominated the Movement and would continue to do so for the next several years. This new philosophy, which became known as cultural nationalism or revolutionary nationalism, went beyond the mere search for civil rights.

Gonzales challenged the young people to see themselves not as a minority group but as a people with a distinct name, language, history, and culture. He helped give new meaning to the word "Chicano," which had long been a derogatory term among many Mexican Americans. It no longer identified lumpen elements, nor did it simply mean a Mexican born on the U.S. side of the border. The term Chicano brought with it a connotation of political awareness and cultural rejuvenation. *Chicanismo* reverberated with militancy and cultural pride.[24] This creation of a new Mexican American proved profoundly important. Rudolfo Anaya, describing this type of event, wrote, "The ceremony of naming, or self-definition, is one of the most important acts a community performs. . . . The naming coalesces the history and values of the group, provides an identification necessary for its relationship to other groups, . . . and most important, the naming ceremony restores pride and infuses renewed energy. . . . [It] creates a real sense of nation, for it fuses the spiritual and political inspirations of a group and provides a vision of the group's role in history."[25] Gonzales understood that the youthful activists were seeking a redefinition of their status, as well as new heroes, and that they aspired to place themselves within the family of national groups. His greatest accomplishment at the conference was to offer them a national identity.

Gonzales gave them a spiritual and political homeland, *Aztlán*—the land from which the Aztecs had migrated to build their great Tenochtitlán. This mythical land lay north of Mexico City, and some Chicano scholars argued that Aztlán was the modern-day Southwest.[26] Gonzales, unconcerned with geography, declared the Southwest to be Aztlán and challenged the activists to reclaim their homeland. Chicanos, he insisted, had a psychological attachment to their land, and the Anglo-Americans had stripped them of it to induce a cultural self-destruction that the barrios were facing. Divested of their land, their dignity, and their history, and prevented from making economic gains, Chicanos had become easy prey for Anglo-American racists and Mexican American "sell-outs."

Aztlán became a battle cry, for it represented Chicano roots that extended deep in the history of the land. This land was the land of the ancestors, and those who crossed the river came not as strangers but as the sons and daughters of the former Aztecs, seeking to reclaim what was once theirs. Gonzales knew that the concept of Aztlán went beyond the political or even historical. It was mythical in proportions and it had to be, to give Chicanos the collective strength to overcome the obstacles of poverty, assimilation, violence, and self-doubt they faced daily. Luis Leal, a literary critic, later wrote, "That is the way it must be for all Chicanos: whosoever wants to find Aztlán, let him look for it, not on the maps, but in the most intimate parts of his being."[27]

From the Chicano Youth Liberation Conference came one of the most significant documents produced by the Chicano Movement, and the one that set the tone for Chicanos' cultural nationalism. "El Plan Espiritual de

Aztlán" embodied much of the nationalist passion of the period. In it Gonzales sought to bring together all the diverse feelings the young activists
brought with them to Denver and to transcend the search for civil rights
with a search for a spiritual nationhood. "In the spirit of a new people," be-
gins the document, "we, the Chicano inhabitants . . . of Aztlán . . . declare
that . . . we are free and sovereign to determine those tasks which are justly
called . . . by our hearts. Aztlán belongs to those who plant the seeds, water
the fields, and gather the crops. We are a Nation, we are a union of free
pueblos, we are Aztlán." [28]

The Plan had four basic points or principles. First, it proclaimed the use
of nationalism as the organizational glue that would bind together all "religious, political, class, and economic factions." Unlike a number of Marxist-
oriented activists who came later, Gonzales understood that most Chicanos
sought unity among all classes. Although most Chicanos knew that acculturated, well-to-do Mexican Americans had normally sided politically against
them, they also knew that their numbers were small. Most Mexican Americans still faced discrimination and prejudice. And most Mexican Americans
were either part of the working class or barely one generation removed. Re-
alistically, the Mexican American community could hardly pull itself out of
its difficulties without the help of the student class and the small progressive middle class composed of college faculty, lawyers, social workers, government employees, skilled workers, and small businessmen. But more important, the Plan Espiritual de Aztlán sought to activate a movement for
national liberation and not just a social revolution.

Scholars and activists who have criticized Gonzales for lacking class
consciousness have ignored the fact that he sought, as did many other Chicano activists, a separate political entity within this country. Although Gonzales may have been romanticizing the abilities of the Chicano people to
free themselves, his views were consistent with the premises of most
national-liberation movements that required class collaboration until the final victory was achieved. Gonzales, in essence, wanted a unity based on culture and national origin rather than on class interests, though he believed
that the dominant ideals were generated from the experiences of the working class. [29] His experience in the harsh urban barrios of Denver imbued his
nationalism with leftist tendencies. Before many other Chicanos, he be-

came a strong supporter of Latin American nationalist and socialist political movements.

Nationalism meant rediscovering, promoting, and maintaining those cultural characteristics that came from the grassroots level. Chicanos had to preserve the *familia* as a social entity and not succumb to the decay of urban life. The barrio needed to return to its role as a communal refuge from the sterility of the Anglo-American world. The music and literature needed to reflect positive aspects of the people in order to overcome the sense of inferiority that many Chicanos felt. Gonzales's nationalism sought to turn back time and to slow down the urbanization of the Chicano family, which he saw as leading to broken homes, parents who could not control their children, and rebellious youth who found camaraderie and family in gangs.[30] It attempted to bring back a way of life romanticized by the older Mexican Americans alarmed by the breakdown of the barrio. This nationalism had strains of conservative populism that, in time, proved unpopular among some Chicano liberals and leftists caught up in the "radical chic" social environment.[31]

Organizational goals constituted the second point of the Plan Espiritual. These related to control of the barrio's educational, economic, and judicial institutions; the development of self-defense mechanisms in the barrios; and the strengthening of the people's cultural values. And they included a political response to American society. From this point came the idea of an independent political party that would contest elections at the local, regional, and national levels. In places where the party could win, election campaigns would be conducted in a serious manner with strategies that could provide victories. In places where Chicanos were a small minority, as in Colorado, the party would be a pressure group, a gadfly in the ear of the political establishment that would allow Chicanos to funnel their energy into political causes.[32] The party—at this stage without a name—would serve as a vanguard, providing structure, a political platform, and a public entity that represented and promoted the Movement. The party would also serve as a way by which Chicanos could remain active in the electoral process without voting or supporting either of the political monster's two heads.

Gonzales, who had headed the Viva Kennedy clubs in Colorado, had seen the ability of political campaigns to arouse the passions and energies of the people. Few political activities had created such a stir in the Mexican American barrios than the presidential bid of the young Irish Catholic from Massachusetts, who took his campaign to the Southwest. After his election, a picture of John F. Kennedy hung next to that of the Virgen de Guadalupe in many humble Mexican American homes.[33] If Chicanos reacted that way to an Anglo-American politician, Gonzales believed that they would rally around a Chicano party with even more enthusiasm.

The third point of the Plan stressed action—numerous activities that promoted the Plan and that worked toward developing defense committees and creating the party. The fourth point encompassed the spirit of the Movement and called for a nation "autonomously free" that would "make its own decisions on the usage of our lands, the taxation of our goods, the utilization of our bodies for war, the determination of justice (reward and punishment), and the profit of our sweat."[34] The Plan inspired intense discussion of the history of Chicanos and their role in contemporary society. The discussion continued for almost a decade. It provided a starting point for the organizational strategies and philosophical underpinnings of numerous groups. And despite the Plan's controversial nature, no profound political discussion occurred without a reference to the Colorado document.

Women played a significant role in these politics of Aztlán. In Colorado, as in Crystal City and throughout the Southwest, women proved hard to intimidate in the political process. They worked hard and often brought the organizational skills that many male activists lacked. Also, the participation of women in Denver served to challenge the men to be *machos* and join the struggle. Activists like Gonzales often used the presence of women to taunt Chicanos into becoming "men" and fighting for *la causa*. The use of symbolism from the Mexican Revolution placed the women in the role of fighters such as *la rielera* (women in the Mexican Revolution), Juana Gallo, and other women made famous in revolutionary *corridos*.[35] For young Chicanas, this role provided a sense of independence and importance that often seemed missing in the traditional role of Mexican women. Their large numbers, and their intense involvement, brought them a measure of respect that they found in few other places. They quickly became the directors, teachers, and main artists of the Crusade for Justice's school, theater, and dance group.

There were two views of Chicanas in the Movement. Those who were married and emphasized their role as wives and mothers were praised for their commitment to the family and for being the transmitters of culture. They represented selflessness, stability, and spirituality within the barrio. The more independent and political Chicanas, on the other hand, represented the "new" women. Often relating better to men than other Chicanas did, these women obtained respect and leadership mobility based on their aggressiveness. These were the women who traveled to conferences along with the men, who participated in the more militant activities, and who often came into conflict with the more chauvinistic males in the Movement. There was room for these women at the highest level of the Movement, but the price to pay was harder work and the necessity of a more aggressive attitude than even that of many of the men. These women were seen as exceptional and necessary, but many activists continued to see them as an aberration from the more traditional Chicana of Aztlán. Welcomed in the heat of battle, they nonetheless represented a challenge to the solidarity of the Movement.[36] The challenge came not only with their presence, but with their ideas on equality and their priorities. Although many Chicanas went along with the extolling of the *familia*, they did so while demanding a redefinition of family roles. They constantly reminded Chicano activists that women of the Mexican Revolution did not just follow "their men" but actually led them into battle and fought. Willingness to do all that men did gave women status in the Movement, though it was status that they had to be vigilant to maintain.

The Crusade for Justice's political agenda attempted to be all-encompassing but should best be noted for having promoted the ideals of cultural nationalism and for having sponsored the Chicano liberation conferences, La Raza Unida Party in Colorado, and numerous other conferences and activities that highlighted La Raza's plight and Chicanos' willingness to struggle to improve it. The Crusade for Justice eventually became overly sectarian and consequently alienated from other Chicano organizations.[37] But its rhetoric, its documents, and its historic confrontations with the mainstream political and social structure guaranteed its place as one of the precursor organizations of the Movement and possibly the main contributor to the hodgepodge of ideas that gained prominence during the Movement's heydays. The Crusade best expressed the rhetorical yearnings of the Movement.

The third significant organization in the Movement, La Raza Unida

Party, arose in Texas. To understand the rise of the party it is necessary to understand the development of Mexican American politics in the state of Texas where it originated. Mexican Americans in Texas seemed to have been the first to become involved in social reforms at the organizational level. At the turn of the century, most of the organizational activity came from mutual-aid societies, labor unions, and workers' associations. These were predominantly working-class organizations. By the 1920s, middle-class groups responded to the growing discrimination against native-born Mexicans. As mentioned in chapter 1, the League of United Latin American Citizens, or LULAC, began in 1929 with the intention of helping Mexican Americans integrate into mainstream society and achieve equal status. Although LULAC organizers avoided direct political partisanship, much of their work had political connotations. Their first efforts involved the development of an organizational creed that served as the guide for the betterment of the Mexican American community. They worked extensively to organize chapters throughout Texas and to link together much of the natural leadership from around the state. Before World War II, Mexican American reformers were tenacious in exposing the harsh treatment of Mexican Americans, but they found little judicial or legislative support for their cause.[38]

By the end of the war, many of the returning G.I.'s who had been in LULAC or had been influenced by the organization came back with desires to expand the reform movements. Many of them, unhappy with LULAC's low-key approach, helped found the American G.I. Forum in 1948. Led by Hector P. García, a medical officer in the war, these men now felt they had a moral obligation to demand their rights, not only as American citizens but as veterans who had risked their lives for their country.[39] These men considered themselves American in every respect. They no longer looked toward the Mexican consuls or government to help them achieve their equal status. They saw their main recourse as going through the judicial system.

Lawyers for the American G.I. Forum united with their colleagues from LULAC to launch a sustained legal charge against discriminatory laws and practices in Texas. Much of the de jure discrimination fell during their legal crusade.[40] But because these organizations depended on legal maneuverings and sought to remain law abiding, they were unsuccessful in forcing changes in recalcitrant school districts, municipal governments, and judicial courts. They often did not have the strength of numbers, nor the belligerency of community activists, to force changes. Although they led school boycotts and held impressive rallies, they had no strategies for a sustained popular movement against discrimination. For those Mexican Americans who survived racist school systems and had the resources to get an education or develop a vocational skill, the efforts of these middle-class reformers proved beneficial. These reformers benefited from a system willing to accommodate the best and the brightest—usually the most acculturated—of the Mexican American community. With time, the fervor of many reformers waned as the deeper problems of economic exploitation and institutional racism became more difficult to solve, and as their own circumstances became more comfortable.[41] There were those, however, who continued the struggle, but now in the electoral arena. Manuel C. Gonzales ran for state representative in 1948; Gus García ran for the board of trustees in San Antonio in 1947, and Henry B. González would begin his rise in Texas politics in the early 1950s. The Viva Kennedy campaign, the 1957 campaign of Richard Tellez in El Paso, PASSO's activity in Crystal City, and the 1964 governor's race in Texas aroused political interest among Mexican Americans. With time, as noted before, Mexican Americans became disillusioned with the limited progress they made in Texas politics, and in the overall social and economic stagnation of the *tejano* community. Because Mexican Americans in Texas had had a tradition of electoral politics, albeit a limited one, the Chicano response in Texas became an electoral one. This led to the rise of La Raza Unida Party.

Enough has been written on the founding of the party to disperse with a detailed history here.[42] Rather, a review of what the party sought to accomplish and what it did accomplish while in power will be discussed. No other Movement organization had as many chapters and as many identifiable leaders as the *partido*.[43] For many Anglo-Americans, the party became the most threatening political organization of the Chicano Movement because it sought to displace them from power and to restructure the American political system. It was separatist in orientation, if not in practice, and for a time it seemed capable of attracting thousands to an open electoral and social rebellion on a scale never before seen among the so-called passive Mexicans of the Southwest.[44]

La Raza Unida Party arose as a direct result of Gutiérrez's activities in the Mexican American Youth Organization (MAYO) that he helped found in

1967. This organization differed from the traditional Mexican American organizations, which sought large memberships composed of older men and women from the community. MAYO instead recruited young men and women who had proved to be natural leaders, who were capable of surviving on minimal resources, and who required only nominal training. They looked for young people susceptible to nationalistic ideals and unattracted by the glitter of American society.[45] Once these men and women were recruited, they were encouraged to go back to their communities to become involved in issues such as the delivery of social services, discrimination, police brutality, political underrepresentation, and education. These men and women recruited other young people and created protest committees that developed a list of demands and an implementation strategy. The main organizational technique proved to be polarization.[46] MAYO quickly spread throughout the state and eventually became involved in several major protests and demonstrations, including over thirty school boycotts. These boycotts were aimed at the heart of what MAYO organizers believed to be the most racist institutions in the state: schools. From these school conflicts came many of the leaders that directed La Raza Unida Party. When the party was founded in Crystal City in 1970, MAYO slowly faded as most Texas activists jumped at the idea of an independent political party.[47]

The electoral victory of 1970 in Crystal City provided activists in the Chicano Movement the first opportunity to put into practice the concept of self-determination and Chicano liberation. Bureaucrats, clerks, teachers, administrators, policemen, and a host of other governmental and educational professionals lost their jobs and were replaced by Chicanos sympathetic to the new party. Within a short period of time, the schools became the main proponents of *chicanismo*, where army recruiters were unwelcome, only UFW lettuce was eaten, the bands played "Jalisco" as their fight song, and Chicano students learned the "real" history of the Southwest. They started graduating in larger numbers and going on to college. The schools also employed a large number of the party's faithful and provided funds to promote their nationalism through activities in the classroom, school plays, and assemblies, as well as through the buying of Chicano books for school libraries. In less than a year, the school, once a symbol of Anglo-American control, became the first exhibit of La Raza Unida Party's blueprint.[48]

The new party allowed Chicanos to control their own political destiny. Chicanos wrote their own platforms, nominated their own candidates, and carried out their own agendas when elected.[49] Gutiérrez believed that coalitions with Anglo-Americans always required Chicanos to give up their most passionate demands. La Raza Unida Party, if successful in winning elections in predominantly Chicano areas, would control twenty-six counties in Texas, mostly South Texas, and would provide Chicanos a tremendous amount of leverage in state and national politics.[50]

The city government set out to provide services to the Chicano barrios that had often been neglected. The Raza Unida administrators went after federal funds and provided paved streets, put up street lights, and remodeled decrepit housing. Parks were built to provide recreational opportunities for the Chicano community and a place for political rallies. When Gutiérrez won the election for county judge in 1974—the highest administrative and judicial office in the county—the new government's sensitivity expanded to the county residents. Court sessions, at the city and county level, were conducted in Spanish, and proved to be more lenient toward Chicanos in passing out sentences and probations.[51] The courts were also used to harass nonsupportive Mexican Americans and political opponents and to intimidate Anglo-American farmers and businessmen who formed the core of the opposition. With this new power came a more confident and at times belligerent attitude on the part of Chicanos in their dealings with Anglo-Americans. In every civic arena, Anglo-Americans were either replaced by new appointees through elections or simply harassed long enough and hard enough until they left. Crystal City, or "Cristal," was the mecca of *chicanismo*, and Anglo-Americans, especially those who were not sympathetic to the party, were not welcome.

Cristal became a powerful symbol of the Chicano Movement. Unlike the activities of middle-class Mexican American reformers, the election of Chicano militants meant demonstrative change. It meant a Chicano agenda that put Chicanos first with little regard to Anglo-American reaction. Cristal embodied much of what Chicanos wanted. Chicano activists sought empowerment, and the capture of the city, school, and county governments ensured part of that. They wanted their culture, language, and history to be taught and promoted by the schools and government, and it was. The schools established bilingual education from kindergarten through twelfth grade, and much of the business of the schools and government was conducted in Spanish or bilingually. Party activists also wanted economic development in the barrios, and here they were only partly successful. They provided patronage through school, city, and county jobs and through contracts with minority businesses. They also attempted several economic development projects. Most were unsuccessful, however, because of the lack of funds.[52] The control of the city and county meant that Chicanos enforced the law, designed the tax rate, prosecuted tax delinquents, set utility rates, and hired the personnel for jobs in the city, county, and school districts. Only those willing to pledge loyalty to the *partido* could benefit directly from the spoils of victory. This loyalty requirement went beyond that of former politicians who simply sought to stay in office. Chicanos in Crystal City wanted to transform the town's politics and social climate from that of a sleepy town run by Anglo-Americans to one of a Chicano utopia, where Chicanos and their culture were firmly entrenched.

For Chicanas, Crystal City became a controlled environment where they assumed roles beyond clerks, fund raisers, and food makers. They took over much of the leadership of the community group Ciudadanos Unidos, they ran for political office and won, they administered several of the city agencies, and they met together and discussed their role as women in Aztlán. Given an opportunity to participate, many proved more than capable of holding their own politically and philosophically against the less progressive men. Because many of them were mothers and housewives, they could not be intimidated with the loss of a job, and this allowed a number of them to be more aggressive politically than their husbands. One of Gutiérrez's major strengths proved to be the loyalty of many of the women in Crystal City. They tipped the balance of power in Ciudadanos Unidos toward him. When he lost a large part of that support, he lost his hold on the county and eventually the city.[53]

Although there were activists who did not like government funding, who wanted to drop the English language altogether, or who wanted a declaration of independence, most Chicano activists and nonactivists took pride in Crystal City. They flaunted it as a product of the efforts of every Chicano who challenged Anglo-American society. Like the poem *Yo Soy Joaquín,* the political manifesto the Plan Espiritual de Aztlán, and the UFW flag, Cristal became a symbol of the Chicano struggle for liberation. In areas outside of

Texas, the party provided an alternative choice for those disillusioned with the traditional parties. And it served as a training ground for many community activists, including those who eventually returned to the mainstream parties.

La Raza Unida Party helped Chicanos learn about the electoral system. It gave them an opportunity to run for office, to write platforms, and to govern when elected. Even while harassed by state law enforcement agencies and Anglo-American citizens' groups, these Chicano politicians learned to mingle with non-Chicano politicians and government bureaucrats in their capacity as elected officials. By representing the "government," they provided Mexican Americans with a sense of empowerment. During a student walkout in Robstown, busloads of students, parents, school administrators, and city officials from Crystal City arrived to add their support. The buses entered the staging areas escorted by Crystal City police cars with officers carrying shotguns. Said Guadalupe Youngblood, years later, "We were shocked and impressed to have the *chota* (law) on our side."[54]

Gutiérrez, at the height of the party's power, claimed that the concept of Chicano power would become a reality only if Chicanos looked to themselves for answers. Rather than foreign ideologies such as socialism and Marxism, Gutiérrez sought to promote the concept of *carnalismo,* or brotherhood, as the Chicano ideology.[55] He would later refer to this *carnalismo* as progressive nationalism. This concept was not so much an ideology as a series of ideas on the nature of being Chicano. *Carnalismo*, like *chicanismo* or cultural nationalism, only made sense in the context of an oppressed people fighting for self-determination. The rhetoric of La Raza Unida Party, as well as that of the Crusade and the UFW, often developed in the heat of battle. This rhetoric contributed to the political ethos of a community in struggle. In the context of rhetoric, or written manifestations such as the Plan Espiritual de Aztlán, *chicanismo* could mean most things to most activists and their followers. Most important, politics in the realm of rhetoric escaped contradictions and conflicts. Only when the rhetoric became practical application did conflicts arise among activists of a nationalist bent. Unity, a political state-of-being often conditioned by the politics of a particular area, served as the first level of unsophisticated ideology. It was one of those political abstractions that never really found a definition but that served as a rallying cry.

La Raza Unida Party's political importance went beyond the elections in Crystal City and the gubernatorial campaigns that shocked traditional politicians. From their party activism, the Mexican American community developed a political instinct. Politics became a daily concern, a legitimate form of protest, and, in the long term, the most effective way to become empowered. Election to office, even when it meant isolation from the political mainstream, provided a forum, an office, staff, money, and constituency. Political involvement, like Chicano art, became a Movimiento icon that would transcend the social movement itself. Before the rise of the *partido*, politics among Mexican Americans were important only during election time, and involvement meant choosing the best Anglo-American candidate. Politics rarely meant fundamental changes. They usually translated into political crumbs, small favors, insignificant appointments, or a reprieve from harassment. The politics of La Raza Unida Party changed that attitude, even after it was gone. After the demise of the Chicano third party, many Mexican Americans continued their electoral participation. The politics of the party inspired a wholesale rise of Mexican American candidates in the traditional parties, particularly the Democratic Party. No strategy of the Movement proved as beneficial or lasting as the electoral strategy of La Raza Unida Party. Few organizations had the opportunity to put into practice their politics as it did. Because of this, La Raza Unida Party became the most important breeding ground for a Chicano polity.

There were other organizations whose rhetoric and actions became symbolic of a community in struggle and that added to the ideas circulating among Mexican Americans. Although these groups were not as significant as the aforementioned, they nonetheless served to politicize the atmosphere of the barrios. The Brown Berets, a Chicano paramilitary group composed mostly of young men (and some women), many of them lumpen elements, had a distinct presence in the barrio. Self-proclaimed policemen of the Movement, they added militancy and stridency to the rallies and protest marches as they provided security and crowd control. They wore army fatigues and brown berets and were best known for their sloganeering. They were successful in attracting working-class youth from both the inner city and the small rural communities. Their newspaper, *Regeneración,* attempted to pattern itself after the famous syndicalist, anarchist newspaper of the Mexican Revolution, though the organization never quite developed an ideology beyond stridency and talk of revolution. The Brown Berets were one of the first organizations to agitate against the police departments, which they accused of constant brutality against young Mexican American males. Patterned somewhat after the Black Panther Party, the Brown Berets were a reminder of the violence that threatened to explode.[56] In the strategy of Aztlán, they were the storm troopers, the masses at the gate that often made it easier for the less militant organizations to negotiate with mainstream officials who feared the alternative. Because the media generally focused on the more extreme groups, the stereotype was created of the violent Chicano activist.

There were organizations that went beyond the Brown Berets' militancy. These were the liberation groups or fronts. The Chicano Liberation Front, the Zapata Liberation Front, the August Twenty-third Movement, and other smaller groups advocated self-defense or violence and became involved in acts of sabotage. These groups worked in the barrio underground and often directed their anger against law enforcement agencies and business establishments that they believed exploited the barrio. Although the actual number of violent acts was small, they were a constant topic in the Chicano newspapers and fueled the passions of the most extreme sector of Chicano activists.[57] Another type of organization was the "defense committees," usually formed to defend activists accused of violating the law. Few of these committees raised the funds necessary for a legitimate judicial defense, so they concentrated on publicizing issues of discrimination, police brutality, and poverty and on recruiting interested Chicanos to the Movement. Both the liberation groups and the defense committees were urban phenomena and involved working-class and lumpen young men greatly alienated from American society. These committees usually were formed on behalf of those Chicanos so low on the social ladder that even most Movimiento organizations did not advocate on their behalf. These individuals lived on the margins of society or had criminal records and had exhibited antisocial behavior. Many were *pintos* serving time for a variety of crimes. In the context of the fringes of the Movimiento, they became political prisoners suffering the oppression of a racist society. And there were a number of times when this seemed an accurate assessment.

The smaller organizations that had a longer lasting effect were the ones formed by Chicanas.[58] These organizations often developed as auxiliaries to male-dominated groups or in reaction to them. They were founded to give women an opportunity to discuss issues relevant to them as a gender group and to keep them involved in the Chicano Movement. In these groups, they provided traditional organizational and fund-raising assistance, planned activities, and served as leaders. And just as important, these groups provided women with a forum in which to participate in the feminist dialogue about the role of women in the Movement and in the home. Enriqueta Longeaux y Vásquez declared that "when we talk of equality in the Mexican American Movement, we better be talking about total equality, beginning right where it all starts, at home."[59]

Many of the founders of these groups were women who had previous experience in organizing. They had already confronted male activists who were reluctant to address women's issues, and so they were prepared to deal with male hostility.[60] Once they joined the Movement, these women became part of the core of activists writing manifestos and party platforms and running for office. They were responsible for the antisexist statements in the platforms of La Raza Unida Party in California, and in Texas they helped write the organizing principles of the party, calling "for the participation of women, including in the decision-making positions within the party, [to] be actively continued through political education, and recruitment of women."[61] They were responsible for organizing women in the fields for the UFW, and they directed most of the cultural education programs of the Crusade for Justice. In each of the organizations in which they participated, they encountered strong male resistance, especially in ideological and leadership matters. Many Chicano activists, caught up in the *machismo* of cultural nationalism, kept seeing the women's role as a complementary one, rather than that of an equal. Others saw them only influencing their men "under the covers."[62] But the Chicana activists persisted, and in 1976 they elected María Elena Martínez as chairperson of La Raza Unida Party in Texas and captured five of the eight contested offices in the bastion of *chicanismo*, Crystal City.[63] More important, these women contributed heavily to the political culture. The male activists came to rely on the image of the Chicana as a *soldadera* for the Movement and became accustomed to speaking a language of inclusion. This created an even greater expectation from Chicanas recruited to the Movement, which in turn emboldened them to demand greater equality. In the process, Chicanas found many Chicanos supportive. Said Martha Cotera, a Raza Unida organizer and candidate, "Most of the time we got what we wanted in the party. They [the male leaders] were very supportive."[64]

The women's groups attracted female activists, students, and professionals willing to work for the women in the barrios, but usually they did not attract working-class women in large numbers. This probably happened because the women's groups tended to be led by highly educated women whose aggressiveness or lifestyles intimidated or alienated working-class women. The working-class women tended to see the oppression of their community in terms of color and ethnicity rather than gender. Many of the working-class women who did participate in the Movement acted much like union women had done in the past in those mostly male organizations— often subsuming their more "female" issues for the overall cause or forcing the men to view the women's issues as part of the family issues of La Raza. These working-class women would serve as a counterbalance to some Chicana feminists who flirted with white radical feminism and its abhorrence of men, familial responsibilities, and culture. The concern over the lives of working-class women would form the basis for Chicana feminism. Working-class Chicanas participated heavily in integrated Movimiento groups such as Raza Unida chapters, Familias Unidas, Barrios Unidos, Chicanas Unidas, and numerous other groups throughout the Southwest and Midwest.

The role of women in the Movement may well have been influenced by the role of women in the numerous revolutionary movements throughout the Third World, and particularly by the popular perceptions of the Mexican *soldadera*. Those organizations, and the individual women who promoted women's issues over those of *la causa,* were often branded as *agringadas.* Yet, in spite of the opposition of many males, the women in the Movement participated actively and acquired numerous skills. Many of them were also able to gain the respect of their male counterparts because they put in as much time as they did and sacrificed as much or more for the cause. Through the Movement and through their participation in Chicana groups, many of them gained the desire to continue on with their studies. They also developed personal and group networks useful to them and their community.[65]

Much has been written about the struggle between the "loyalists"— those committed to cultural nationalism—and the feminists.[66] The conflict was real and at times bitter. But it was not a fight between feminists and antifeminists, but rather a fight over strategy and tactics. "Loyalists" supported most of the feminist issues of the day and constantly fought against the party's sexism. But they saw the struggle as one of community, not as one of individuals or gender groups. For many of them—at this stage of their feminist development—the first discrimination they faced was due to their ethnicity and not their gender. It is easy to scoff at that analysis as shortsighted or superficial, but during the Movement most Chicano and Chicana activists saw the struggle in terms of nationality. Those who rejected this premise were those who had begun to construct their own Movement paradigm that envisioned Chicanas participating in all aspects of the struggle. This participation, however, did not limit itself to organizational or political functions but extended into the ideological domain. They were interested in understanding the Chicano experience not as extensions of the men but as what they uniquely were: working-class women of mixed blood. The concentration on the "Chicana" experience pushed them toward a separatist female orientation that did not fit into the cultural nationalism of the male leadership. This threatened some male leaders' constructs of the community. Because of this, the women were privately and publicly attacked as lacking commitment to La Raza and as being "women libbers" chasing after the American dream of their white sisters. They came to be branded as the *viejas,* the wenches of the Movement who had betrayed the cause and divided the struggle between gender groups.[67] The feminist Chicanas would prove to be right in much of their assessment of the Movement's sexism, but they would also cease to be a major influence in the Chicano community at large. These Chicana feminists would eventually adopt the more nationalist line of the "loyalists" in their own struggle with white feminists.

Those Chicanas who remained, at least up through the early stages of the demise of the Movement, were those who moved on to positions of leadership in the Movement. As some of the male leaders began to defect from Movement organizations, the women's role became more important. Because they came into their own during later stages of the Movement, many of them were able to make the transition to Hispanic reform organizations that would arise after the decline of Chicano activism. These women helped the Movimiento to be less sexist than the New Left and the Black Power

Movement, both of which failed to integrate women's platforms into their organizations.

Also influential in the Movement were the numerous Marxist and socialist groups that arose quite early in the Movement, particularly in California. At first sympathetic and then progressively more critical of cultural nationalism, these organizations deviated from the more nationalistic agenda and sought to bring a class analysis to the struggle. Only one of the many Marxist organizations—CASA–Hermandad General de Trabajadores—ever developed much of a following, but they nonetheless added to the Chicano dialogue, particularly that which dealt with class. CASA promoted a view that Chicanos were just another part of the Mexican working class. Through their popular newspaper, *Sin Fronteras,* they galvanized support for undocumented workers and pushed the Movement—which they considered at times reactionary because it lacked a clear class philosophy—toward a militant position on immigration issues.[68] CASA's astute leadership and its disciplined membership seemed capable of providing cohesion and a more defined ideology to the Movement. But CASA never considered itself a Chicano organization, and its constant criticism of the Movement alienated it from other Chicano groups. Eventually, its failure to coopt the Movement led to internal schisms and its demise. Other, more mainstream leftist organizations, such as the American Communist Party and the Socialist Workers Party, as well as different variations of Marxists, *guevarristas*, Stalinists, and others, contributed to the debate on the Chicano experience and even to the debate on a homeland. These organizations sought to provide a scientific approach to Chicano ideology. They all failed to develop a consensus, but they, like CASA, contributed much to the ideas of the Chicano Movement.[69]

It was the direct action of these groups that added the final phase to the development of a Chicano militant ethos. The Chicano organizations attempted to "operationalize" their rhetoric, and partly succeeded. That is, the rhetoric of the rallies, protest marches, and impromptu debates became the basis for many of the platforms, manifestos, and operational strategies of the Movement. Ideas often arose from political action, were tested through their rhetorical use, and then either gained acceptance and popularity or proved uninspiring. Those that gained acceptance among a core of activists then became part of the pool of ideas from which activists formulated their political strategies.[70] This is not to say that Chicano activists did not study, write, or discuss ideas. They most certainly did. In fact, they spent much time debating ideas. But few wrote enough political theory for it to become a basis for an ideology. Chicanos, following the oral tradition of their communities, "thought out loud," and in the arena of public discourse refined political strategy.

Beyond the Plan Espiritual de Aztlán, only CASA's Marxist polemics were a significant mass of ideas. CASA's ideology, however, never caught on with the majority of activists. Most were cultural nationalists who distrusted foreign ideologies, notwithstanding their own admiration for socialist national-liberation movements. Chicano political strategy developed as Chicano activists publicly debated the problems the Mexican American community encountered. They created a dialogue that encompassed numerous ideas on race, class, historical experience, and Chicano culture. This dialogue, when interpreted similarly by numerous organizations, created a semblance of national ideology but, when reduced to regional or local application, remained a loosely constructed strategy that linked groups nationally but never subsumed their regional differences.

Kingsville was one community to be affected by much of the rhetoric and political strategies circulating at the time. The Chicano activists there were *gutierristas,* or adherents of Gutiérrez, and they sought a duplication of the Crystal City takeover. The strategy of the Kingsville activists became a mixture of those of the major Chicano organizations mentioned earlier, and the political activity in Kingsville went through the four phases of the Chicano Movement.

Gutiérrez had attended Texas A & I University in the mid-1960s and while there formed a chapter of PASSO for young Mexican Americans.[71] During his time at Texas A & I, his activism was much like that of the middle-class reformers. It involved raising people's consciousness about the needs of the community and working for moderate Mexican American candidates. Those who came after him became involved in MAYO politics and eventually became members of La Raza Unida Party. When they did, they formed La Raza Unida Club at the university. The club controlled student politics through most of the decade of the 1970s, although its real purpose was to provide resources for the activists seeking to organize Kingsville for the party.

The Ethnic Studies Center became a gathering place for planning Movimiento activities. These activities were opportunities both to express ethnic pride and to verbally attack Anglo-American institutions and politics. These activities were also meant to bring together the students with members of the community, much in the way Gonzales of the Crusade for Justice wanted to bring barrio youth and college students together. Celebrations of Cinco de Mayo, Diez y Seis de Septiembre, and other fiestas were sponsored by the club, with the use of university resources and facilities, and these events were geared toward attracting the citizens of the Kingsville community. Through participation in these events the students became reacquainted with the barrio, but on a different level. The students were seen as the future leaders of a community in struggle, whereas *la gente* represented the warriors of the past. Class differences were put aside as they all formed a common bond as Chicanos.

University students and staff were used as resource people to teach other students and community people about Chicano history. Courses taught by José Reyna, director of the ethnic studies program, had practical application for students as they went on protest marches, passed out leaflets, assisted the Trabajadores Unidos de Kingsville, and worked as campaign aides for Familias Unidas in nearby Robstown. For this, they received academic credit. Those students found to have valuable skills and a commitment to La Raza were recruited to work with the community activists who were the real leaders of La Raza Unida Club. These new recruits were invited to the three-bedroom house across from the stadium for long *concientización* (consciousness-raising) sessions at night. These sessions became more and more nationalistic as the students progressed in understanding. Once indoctrinated, the students were assigned a special function, and if they proved to be politically sophisticated as well as hard workers, they were invited to the planning meetings and to work on the underground newspaper *El Chile*. Through that process I was introduced to the Movement in Kingsville.

It was after an ethnic studies night class in the fall of 1974 that Reyna approached me. He knew I was a journalism major, and so he asked me to look into the university's employment practices as they related to the maintenance workers, most of whom were Chicano. As an already-motivated student of his ethnic studies class, I jumped at the opportunity. He quickly referred me to the aforementioned house, and that night I spent hours lis-tening to Raul Villarreal and Jorge Guerra talk about the university's em-ployment practices, protest politics, Chicano history, the Mexican Revo-lution, and working-class culture. Much like many young people of my generation, I became fascinated by the new interpretation of Mexican American history, by the bold defiance, and by the excitement of embark-ing on a social movement. I came to believe in the rightness of the farm-workers' struggle and the land-grant movement, I came to accept "Corky" Gonzales's view of our history, and I came to admire Gutiérrez's work in Crystal City and the concept of the third party.

The new view soon led me and other recruits to see the Mexican Amer-ican middle class as archaic in its thinking because of its refusal to let go of the politics of accommodation. We often chided them in meetings and in the underground newspaper. Unable to respond to our criticism, middle-class Chicanos at the university, or in city politics, attempted to steer clear of us or, that failing, to be on good terms with us by providing valuable informa-tion on university or city policies and by making monetary donations to our cause. Some even attempted cooption by inviting us to their meetings and exhorting us to join their political campaigns. But our mistrust remained firm even when some individuals became good acquaintances. We tolerated them as the friendly enemy. Despite our dislike for the middle-class Mexi-can Americans, Anglo-American liberals were the main target of our dis-dain. Liberalism symbolized to us, as it did to many other activists, a politics of appeasement rather than change. Anglo-American liberals, we argued, sought to placate Chicanos, not to empower them. We shared the Crusade for Justice's assessment of them: "The Anglo who is sympathetic, who is sincerely interested in la raza . . . must be able to respect us when we say . . . we want to do this on our own. . . . What's happened with some liberals is that when [we] tell them we're having a meeting that they can't come to, they get all uptight. And the next thing you know you have an enemy. And they were probably enemies to begin with."[72]

In Kingsville, we shared a myopic view with other Chicano militant or-ganizations of the time. We saw the Movement in terms of our own commu-nity's needs and interpreted the rhetoric of *chicanismo* in a way peculiar to our South Texas town. Although we had a very small farmworker popula-tion, we continually extolled the virtues of the *campesino* and engaged in support activities for the Texas Farm Workers Union. We sought to tie the Trabajadores Unidos to Chávez's union and to other militant Chicano unions of the past, as well as to union movements in Latin America. With monies from the Student Union Governing Board, we paid Reies López Tijerina to come and speak to the Kingsville community about the land-grant movement in New Mexico. Although most of the land lost by Mexican Americans in Texas had been owned by Mexican elite families, and not communally owned as in New Mexico, we condensed the two experiences to charge Anglo-Americans with a brutal robbery of Chicano lands throughout the Southwest. La Raza Unida Party became our political vehicle and Crystal City our empowerment model. The poem *Yo Soy Joaquín* spoke to our mythical past, and *Occupied America* to our reality. Gutiérrez would be our leader, but only in a statewide or national context. True leadership came from the leaders of La Raza Unida Club, the Trabajadores Unidos, and from the Kingsville working class.[73]

The Movement in Kingsville, like the rest of the Movement, depended on the success or failure of political tactics and strategies. Electoral victories, successful protests, and other activities with positive results brought pride and emboldened us to continue to make demands of the Kingsville power elite. Electoral defeats, unsuccessful protests, and other failures accentuated for us the inequities in society and brought either bitterness and anger or a renewed determination to make changes. The main activities in Kingsville mirrored those of other areas. The core of activists were young, many of them students or former students who had been recruited through the ethnic studies center. They published a community newspaper, ran candidates for office, promoted Chicano culture and arts, pushed a diverse agenda, and leaned in allegiance toward one of the identifiable Chicano national leaders. The Kingsville group's primary goals were to make Chicanos conscious of their history and identity and to provide empowerment to the barrios through education and electoral politics. For Chicanos in Kingsville, amid the heat of political and cultural battles, rhetoric, tactics, and strategies took the place of defined ideologies.

Most Chicano activist organizations that proved even partially successful in making changes in the way Mexican Americans were treated tended to be those that were action oriented and continually putting their strategies into practice. Even the Crusade for Justice, which involved itself with ideology and political dialogue, had a commitment to action and militant tactics. From its alternative school to its defense committees and liberation conferences, the Crusade for Justice continually promoted strategies and action. The farmworkers movement, the land-grant alliance, La Raza Unida Party, and other groups were organizations that evolved in response to their own constant maneuvering, as well as the mainstream's reaction to their activities. Much of the political ethos came from the UFW's grape and lettuce boycotts, Reies Tijerina's Tierra Amarilla raid, the Crystal City takeover, the liberation conferences in Denver, the Chicano Moratorium,[74] and numerous other regional and local tactical activities in which Chicano organizations were engaged. Individuals became committed through the indoctrination they received, but commitment also came from the experience of being politically active. For MAYO, commitment came when its members stood in the picket lines between the hostile law enforcement agencies and the striking farmworkers. In Tucson, Chicanos became committed when they camped out on the barrio land that was to become a golf course for Anglo-Americans and challenged police to remove them. From each struggle came new terms, anecdotes, songs, poems, political slogans, and heroes. These were the essence of political culture. Interpreted by Chicano activists within the context of their local struggles, they formed a part of a larger ethos.

CHAPTER FIVE

The Movement in Robstown

In the preceding chapters I discussed the four-stage process of the Movement and its effect on the political ethos of the larger Mexican American community. That process can also be seen at the local level if we study communities in which the Movement played an influential part. One such community is Robstown, a small agricultural community in South Texas. Robstown was the scene of La Raza Unida Party's last political hurrah outside of Crystal City and is one place where the development of the Movement's ethos can be seen.

Robstown is a fairly new community, having been established in 1906 at the junction of the St. Louis Brownsville Railway and the Mexican National Railway, fifteen miles west of the city of Corpus Christi. The land on which Robstown is located belonged at one time to the Robert Driscoll family, who bought some of the property from Mexican land-grant holders. Daniel O' Driscoll had come to South Texas from Ireland in the 1830s. After serving in the Texas Republic's army, he received 1,280 acres in nearby Victoria County. His son and grandson increased the family property by thousands of acres in the western part of Nueces County. In 1903, Robert Driscoll, his son Robert, Jr., and a number of other farmers incorporated the St. Louis Brownsville Railway to carry their cotton and sorghum to market and to bring people to the region.[1]

By 1907, the Driscoll family had sold much of its land to George H. Paul, a midwesterner, who made his money by providing railroad excursions through Texas and the Midwest. Paul set out to populate the skeletal community known as Robert's Town or Robstown. Soon he had hundreds of Midwest farmers buying land and moving down to South Texas, bringing their culture, politics, and crops.[2] By 1908, the town had a school, and four years later, a charter. Shortly after its founding, Robstown took part in the agricultural revolution that affected much of the South Texas region.[3] Hundreds of Mexican workers came, attracted to the area by the prospect of work in the cotton fields and on the sorghum farms. Their cheap labor provided the impetus for an economic transformation. By the 1920s, the town had eleven cotton gins, and by the mid-1930s Robstown vegetable packers employed over 1,500 Mexican workers to pack the onions, cabbage, spinach, beets, and other vegetables that were shipped out on the eleven trains that passed through the town every twenty-four hours.[4]

Prosperity became a reality for many of the Anglo-American farmers who came to the region. They had profitable crops, political influence, and economic security. Most important, they had the cheap labor that had lured them there in the first place. Other Anglo-Americans became the businesspeople, merchants, and government and school officials of the new town. Because of its late founding, Robstown avoided most of the conflicts that existed in other South Texas communities between the old Anglo-American ranchers and the new farmers.[5] Anglo-American farmers had it much the way they wanted it.

For the Mexican workers, and their Mexican American progeny, that prosperity and economic security eluded them. Most were field workers, packers, and unskilled laborers, and their wives, if not in the fields, were domestic workers. Their lives seemed characterized by poverty, ignorance, and constant discrimination. They were paid less than Anglo-American workers, they were relegated to segregated neighborhoods, and their children were kept out of school. "They depended [on] an exploitative patron system for their basic welfare," reflected a Methodist minister in the 1970s.[6]

As was the case in other places where Mexicans and Mexican Americans were segregated and isolated, the workers in Robstown developed their own internal community. They sold to each other, cooperated in building shacks, shared *hierbas*, and found ways to enjoy life. They attended dances and were entertained by *carpa* shows coming from Mexico and other parts of Texas.[7] Mutual-aid societies were formed to help workers and their families deal with the harsh realities of powerlessness and economic destitution. The societies provided funds for burials and emergencies, and its members taught schooling to Mexican American children who were not allowed into the school system or who worked most of the day in the fields. They provided a building for classrooms and for a library with books in Spanish. From these organizations came many of the organic leaders of the community, especially of that part of the community that did not integrate. Los Hijos de Hidalgo, the largest of the mutual-aid societies, had around 400 members at its strongest.[8]

By the 1940s, some Mexican Americans had left the field work and the packing sheds. Despite segregated schools, they were learning English and acquiring employment skills and even some higher education. A number of these were veterans from World War II who came back to Robstown expecting things to change and willing to make the changes themselves. Armed with the G.I. Bill for schooling and business opportunities, and with a confidence that came with their experience in war, they challenged the condescending and racist attitudes in their communities.[9] They came with a desire to be joiners and participators in the community's affairs. The 1940s and 1950s were years of constant legal challenges to segregation by Mexican Americans, and much activity by groups such as LULAC and the American G.I. Forum. In Robstown, the American G.I. Forum had a presence. Hector P. García, head of the organization, lived in nearby Corpus Christi.

The local chapter of the American G.I. Forum agitated much within the mainstream of Mexican American civic crusades of the period. Its members sought inclusion into the American mainstream and the desegregation of the schools. Their successes, and there were several, increased their commitment to the process, a process that often implied assimilation. The fact that these were the years of the Cold War tempered any radicalism that could have occurred in rural communities like Robstown. But the sheer numbers of Mexican Americans in towns such as Robstown made it easier for some of the returning veterans and their families to integrate into the peripheries of the mainstream. The changing demographics made it necessary for Anglo-American elites to be politically inclusive of a small number of middle-class Mexican Americans who were willing to support a status quo and thus keep change to a minimum. In 1946, Robstown elected its first Mexican American to the school board.[10] Others would slowly follow.

Integration, however, did not mean that Robstown Mexican Americans were willing to ignore the problems of discrimination that confronted them. With integration came—at times—a demand for equal treatment and similar facilities and conditions. They wanted to be treated as "Americans." In 1949, the American G.I. Forum accused the Nueces County schools of blatant segregation. "School board officials are purposely and stubbornly trying . . . to deprive the Latin American children of their god-given rights," stated an American G.I. Forum document. "We as veterans did not fight . . . to come back to our state and live and tolerate such humiliation and suffering of our children."[11] The Robstown veterans were particularly angered because Mexican American children were moved to a newly constructed school, while the Anglo-American children stayed in the old school, thus maintaining segregated school populations. With time, however, desegregation became less a point of contention as the school population became overwhelmingly Mexican American.

By the 1960s, things had simply not gotten much better economically or socially for Mexican Americans. According to the Census of 1960, more than half of the Robstown families lived in poverty. At the time, Mexican Americans made up 72 percent of the total population and nearly all of the poor. Mexican Americans averaged 2.9 years of school. Their median income was $1,678, and their unemployment rate hovered around 15 percent. Forty-three percent of the houses in the barrio were deteriorating, 57 percent had no private bathrooms, and in the unincorporated west side where most Mexican Americans lived, overcrowding prevailed.[12] After years of segregation and economic depression for Mexican Americans, the Robstown community resembled many other South Texas communities where Anglo-Americans dominated the economic, political, and social life of the town. Reading old issues of the *Robstown Record,* the only newspaper in town, it becomes obvious that Mexican Americans were a public nonentity before the 1970s.[13]

The rumblings of activism first appeared in 1970 at the high school. A group calling itself Movimiento Chicano de Robe formed to discuss problems in the schools. The group was concerned with dropout rates, poor counseling, lack of Mexican American teachers, Anglo-American hostility, and lack of bilingual education programs.[14] Composed of students, parents, and social and civic leaders, the group attempted to negotiate with school officials. This group, like many of the early 1960s Mexican American organizations, wanted change through civil negotiation. The fact that the Robstown school board now had five Mexican Americans made it logical to expect change quickly. But they soon found that the new board members were only slightly more attuned to the needs of the Mexican American students than those before them. The new board members approached education in much the same way that the Anglo-American board members had in the past. Keeping the students in line, teaching them citizenship, and promoting the school within the community seemed the principal concerns.

In most of the Mexican American educational reform campaigns of the 1940s and 1950s, desegregation had dwarfed issues such as curriculum, counseling, graduation rates, and discipline. The American G.I. Forum had become the dominant organization in the educational reform struggles. Documents available on the organization's activities point out that two of its main concerns were desegregation of the schools and the hiring of Mexican Americans in the schools.[15] Whereas LULAC leaders had discussed and critiqued the role of schools in educating Mexican Americans, the American G.I. Forum, with its heavy emphasis on patriotism, sought inclusion in the American educational mainstream. To leaders of this organization, the public school system's curriculum was good but exclusive. Consequently, when elected to school boards, many Mexican Americans of this generation concentrated on access but proved devoid of creativity in making curricular changes. Also, as in most small towns, the Anglo-American superintendent of Robstown had tremendous power. He, not the school board, made most of the decisions affecting the children's schooling. The fact that he presided over one of the largest employers in town placed him in a position of much influence in the community.[16]

The group of reformers, unable to make changes, did not remain together long, since many of its members left for the migrant fields in the late spring. This defused their activism. One year later, the students demanded the right to celebrate Cinco de Mayo, and the school administration obliged. The following April, the students walked out of school when their grievances of the past three years continued to be ignored. The list of grievances included more excused absences per year, elimination of the practice of reducing a student's grade because of absences, and no expulsion without prior communication with parents.[17] Students and parents felt that the mostly Anglo-American faculty and administration treated the students with disrespect. According to one freshman student, "They [teachers] say Chicanos are dumb. We are humans too. Just because our color is different, they have no right to call us names and criticize us."[18] Students were convinced to return the next day and wait for a school board hearing on April 10. By this time, MAYO activists, who by then had led boycotts in over 30 schools in the state of Texas,[19] had joined the school controversy.[20]

Four hundred people crowded the meeting room of the board on April 10. The board president quickly threatened to adjourn the meeting if disruptions occurred. The students presented their demands, to which five more had been added: Chicano speakers at school assemblies, an intramural sports program, longer hours for the school library, adequate textbooks, and field trips.[21] The board members promised to investigate each demand but told the crowd it would take at least six weeks to make a decision. In six weeks, the school year would be over. The students demanded immediate action and accused the board of trying to delay until the end of the school year. The board president angrily responded that the board had already voted to investigate. The student leaders simply said, "Walkout tomorrow," and the meeting hall emptied.[22]

The boycotting students congregated in a park called La Lomita. MAYO activists, now deeply involved, advised them to come to the park and stay together with their classmates. There, they would have musical bands, political speeches, food, and instruction by volunteers. Graduate students from Texas A & I University in nearby Kingsville taught Chicano history classes. Said one student, "We learned more about our culture than we had ever known before." At the school, the Mexican American history course was taught in the building-trades room, where the sound of the machines made it hard to hear.[23] A *teatro* group from the Colegio Jacinto Treviño presented skits about the problems in the schools and about problems Chicanos faced in general.

To gather parental support and defuse charges of delinquency or radicalism, the activists organized groups of four to five students to visit homes and explain the walkout. MAYO and Raza Unida party activists expanded the discussion to include grievances that Mexican Americans had long experienced in their relationship with Anglo-Americans. Parents remembered their own school years—the segregation they had faced, the blatant stereotyping, and even the violence. Long-forgotten acts of racism were discussed. Mexican American parents were encouraged to openly discuss their bitterness and resentment and to focus their hurt and anger in the direction of the school administration and the city officials.[24] For Chicano activists, the school boycott served to crystallize a new attitude about the abuses of the past. The activists chipped away at the liberal notion, often promoted by middle-class Mexican Americans, that time and integration would solve the problems of the community. Activists assailed the status quo approach of the board members and pointed out the board's inability to change the "gringo" school policies.

On the third week of the boycott, several busloads of students, parents, and school officials from Crystal City arrived to boost the Robstown Movement's morale. They arrived in official buses led by Crystal City police cars. That impressed Mexican Americans in Robstown, who had never seen the government on their side. The speakers from Crystal City encouraged the students to spread the boycott to unsupportive businesses and exhorted them to establish a chapter of La Raza Unida Party. They also took verbal shots at the Mexican Americans on the school board. "With five Mexican Americans on the school board, it's hard to believe that they can't sit down and talk things out with the students," declared Noe Angel Gonzalez, superintendent of Crystal City schools.[25] In the end, the students were able to get only promises. They had mistimed the boycott by starting it too close to the end of the school year. The student rebellion continued, however, during graduation ceremonies. Several young men with arm bands grabbed their diplomas and clenched their fists in the air. At the recessional, a flag—brown with a black eagle on a golden circle, representing Chicano liberation in Robstown—was unfurled amid cheers from many students and some parents.[26]

Chicano activists, who came to the boycott late, understood it would be difficult to win the school battle. Their goal, then, centered on creating an organization that would challenge the Anglo-American power base and discredit the leadership of the Mexican American middle class. In this they were partly successful with the formation of Familias Unidas. Familias Unidas became the Movimiento organization in Robstown. Composed of families instead of individuals, the organization set in motion the process of the Movement. By becoming the new activist organization in town, it challenged the local chapter of the American G.I. Forum as the advocate for civil rights. It also changed the dialogue from one of integration to one of empowerment. Said one Mexican American letter writer, "Confronting the critical problems of today with effective political, social, and educational reforms is the necessary action. Democratic emotionalism and the deceased Kennedy will not remedy the Chicanos' needs today."[27] The reference to Kennedy was a veiled attack on Mexican American Democrats and their obsession with the Kennedy legacy. Chicano activists were particularly scathing in their criticism of politicians who created a dichotomy between the "good" national Democrats and the "bad" state Democrats in Texas. This dichotomy helped Mexican American reformers pin their hopes on a national liberal leadership that would create change at the local level. For Chicano activists, this "wishful thinking" kept Mexican Americans from taking the responsibility to make changes themselves. It kept them dependent on Anglo-Americans for leadership, ideas, and strategies. It also meant that Chicano activists could not criticize the American political system or challenge entrenched Anglo-American politicians if they were Democrats. The activists were out to condemn Anglo-American society. In a poem titled "Ni Tuyo Ni Mio," Abraham Arevalo wrote, "Esta raza blanca nos ha desgraciado . . . nos ha destrullido nuestra cultura (This white race has disgraced us . . . has destroyed our culture)."[28] In this context, the word *desgraciado* meant more than disgraced. Ruined, denigrated, abused, or destroyed are stronger and more accurate definitions. The Familias Unidas activists attacked what they considered the Anglo-American assault on Mexican culture and the Mexican family. Said one activist, "One of the problems we face is that our families are broken up and destroyed by Anglo values. We also realize that for us to be really successful in changing things, we need the strength, support, and wisdom of our parents."[29]

Familias Unidas, following the MAYO concept of empowerment, became involved in the political process. In 1973, in the first local elections in which they took part, they won three positions on the city council and three on the school board. Familias Unidas concentrated on changing the style and substance of politics in Robstown. The organization did not promote its individual candidates but rather its slate and its platforms. In order to be candidates, members had to go before the group and convince the other members that they best represented the goals of Familias Unidas. Oftentimes, candidates were drafted by the membership and convinced to run for office. The organization discouraged leadership based on personality. "Thou shalt not be a hero," became the motto for the Robstown activists.[30] By choosing its leaders and candidates by consensus, and encouraging discussion, the organization minimized public schisms. In 1975, the organization ran three Baptists for the city government. That would have been unheard of in a Mexican American Catholic community if the members had not already discussed and debated the ramifications.[31] In the process, the organization elevated the issue of Mexican American marginalization to a level that attempted to transcend matters of religion, family relations, and, to some extent, class. Seeing themselves as Mexican Americans with limited individual opportunities, they realized the need to group together. Familial allegiance, political affiliations of the past, and class became secondary to group ascendancy.

Familias Unidas' strength was its familial structure. The structure reflected the Movement's concern with the totality of the community. By admitting only families, the organization could involve and indoctrinate all members of the family with Chicano Movement ideals. The activists idealized the Chicano family as a unit of hardworking people who communicated with and loved each other, thus labeling the "generation gap" as a "decadent gringo problem." Familial involvement kept the youth out of trouble and involved in positive Movement activities, thus preparing them for future leadership. In small towns like Robstown, politicians were elected and leaders selected through familial linkages, which were often unbreakable. By bringing families together, the organization hoped to benefit from the extended family networks and to enlarge those networks by bringing together unrelated families.

Another reason for bringing families together was to emphasize the collective class and racial nature of the Movement in Robstown. Individuals often escaped class identification because their activism, or activist status, allowed them fluidity between classes. They could be economically middle class but intellectually in tune with the working class. They could be working class but have a middle-class education, as was the case with a number of the participants of Familias Unidas. They were teachers, university students, or college graduates working in skilled or semiskilled jobs so they could stay in Robstown and be part of the Movement.[32] Mexican Americans in Robstown were predominantly poor and working class but proud of their families, their neighborhoods, and their "Mexicanness." Bringing the family into the organization intact bonded the militancy of the youth with the cultural roots of the older generation of Mexican Americans. The new problems of youthful alienation from authority, education, and Anglo America meshed with the experiences of their elders with racism, segregation, and cultural denigration. The families became "Chicano families" or *familias mexicanas*. Rather than be marginalized entities of poor Mexican Americans, the families of Familias Unidas became units of activism representing a vibrant barrio in defense of its culture, language, and political space. The concept of the *pueblo* or *la gente* became key to the organizing efforts of the Chicano activists of Robstown and to their politics.

The concept of the Chicano working-class family on the move set in motion the reinterpretation of the Chicano experience in Robstown. Chicano youth and their elders were taught that Anglo-Americans, in coalition with the small Mexican American middle class, conspired to keep them subservient, segregated, and politically powerless. They were reminded that the land around Robstown had once been owned by Mexican Americans and had been stolen by Anglo-Americans through deceit and violence. They were constantly reminded that Mexican culture and customs were ridiculed in school and that students were punished for speaking Spanish, a language most of them used for many of their daily transactions. Yet many in Robstown had resisted assimilation and retained their culture. In the words of "Corky" Gonzales, they had lost the "economic battle [but] won the struggle of cultural survival."[33]

The members of Familias Unidas underwent a constant education on the issues of the Movement. The college-age members who went to Texas A & I University in nearby Kingsville were indoctrinated by the activists of La Raza Unida Club and by the ethnic studies courses they took under José Reyna. The activists used the newspaper *La Lomita,* founded during the school boycotts, as the official organ of the organization. The newspaper served to counter the anti–La Raza sentiments of the *Robstown Record.* It also provided tidbits of history and demythified Anglo-American superiority. Cartoons by "Control," a Robstown artist, ridiculed Anglo and Mexican American politicians and provided a more positive image of the Chicano. Control's defiant cartoons became famous throughout the Movement.

The Robstown Movement became a part of the larger Movement through its participation in the Texas La Raza Unida Party. Guadalupe Youngblood became chairperson of the state party and the Familias Unidas delegation one of the strongest at the state conventions. The activism in Robstown also attracted some of the more prominent members of the Texas Chicano Movement. After the 1974 gubernatorial election, Ramsey Muñiz, the party's candidate, and Carlos Guerra, his campaign manager, moved to Robstown and became part of Familias Unidas. While they brought notoriety to the organization, both learned to conform to the group ideology of collective leadership.[34]

The Familias Unidas activists never won over enough voters to take control of Robstown as others had done in Crystal City, Cotulla, San Juan, and other communities in South Texas. Nevertheless, they engaged in the politics of Aztlán. Their main efforts centered on defending the poor community from tax increases, hiring more Chicanos in the city government and the school district, and defeating the Anglo-American elites who had dominated Robstown politics for years. Familias Unidas activists became aggressive in pursuing criminal prosecution against law enforcement officers who abused their power[35] and in helping poor Mexican Americans caught in the cycle of drug addiction. They also challenged elected officials to focus on the needs of the poor residents of Robstown and less on boosterism. Although not successful in making most of the changes themselves, the Chicano activists nonetheless brought these issues to the forefront, and the issues became part of the community's political dialogue, even among the more moderate Mexican Americans.

In many ways, the political approach of Familias Unidas was a mix of conservative populism and Chicano nationalism. Members of the organization had their weekly meetings but often met daily at their storefront hall. There they worked on the newspaper, made silk-screened T-shirts and posters, discussed politics, and had potluck dinners. They made it a common practice to attend the meetings of the school board, the city council, and the city utilities commission. With their supporters urging them on, elected officials from Familias Unidas transformed routine meetings into extensive sessions with long agendas and much debate.[36] They proposed raises for poor city-school employees and demanded pay cuts for highly placed, mostly Anglo-American bureaucrats and administrators. They promoted an enlarged Chicano studies curriculum in the high school, only to have the board deadlock on the issue and the superintendent reject "that Mexican American junk."[37] They pushed the hiring of Mexican Americans and the dismissal of Anglo-American city officials who had neglected the concerns of Chicanos in the past.

Because Robstown was not a county seat, or even the largest community in the county, Familias Unidas activists knew there were limits to how much change they could make in the political structure of the county. Robstown also had a strong political middle class that resisted Chicano militancy and was quick to red-bait. Said one middle-class leader, "I'm not in agreement with any of [their] socialist or communist ideas at all. When you have a system like the one we have . . . there's really no reason to talk about communism."[38] Being near Corpus Christi meant confronting the American G.I. Forum and its fervent patriots. Robstown activists walked a tightrope politically. They tried coalition activism on issues of police brutality, school segregation, and blatant racism but during election times went it alone against Anglo-American politicians, Mexican American Democrats, and barrio politicians. They were constantly being challenged by Anglo–Mexican American coalitions with names such as Amigos for Progress, Unity Party, and Concerned Citizens of Robstown.[39] Said County Commissioner Solomon Ortíz of the Amigos for Progress, "We couldn't just lay down and let Familias Unidas run over us. We had to do something and we are doing it."[40]

During the elections in 1976, Familias Unidas made its bid to take over the community as had Ciudadanos Unidos in Crystal City and Barrios Unidos in Cotulla. They banked on a strong voter turnout and help from activists in surrounding communities. On election day, the town seemed overrun by Familias Unidas supporters, their posters and bumperstickers, and vehicles with loudspeakers urging La Raza to vote. In the early hours, many activists believed that the town would finally be rid of gringos and *vendidos*. But the opposition's red-baiting, their larger war chest, and their effective absentee-voter strategy handed defeat to the majority of Familias Unidas candidates.[41] It came as a bitter blow to the Familias Unidas activists, who discovered numerous voting irregularities but did not have the resources to engage in a long appeals process. The defeat demoralized the organization, and its numbers slowly dwindled. By 1978, the last Familias Unidas elected officials had resigned.[42]

The activists melted into the community, trying to maintain credibility with those who still felt alienated by those in power and with those who were newly discovering racism and discrimination in the city of Robstown. By the early 1980s, Robstown became a town dominated politically by Mexican Americans. The Mexican American middle class had itself "persuaded" most of the Anglo-American politicians to leave office.[43] The former activists, in conjunction with more aggressive Mexican American reformers, eventually captured control of the school board and "Mexicanized" the school district.[44] They also captured a justice-of-the-peace position. Although still far from being the envisioned utopia, Robstown went from a town dominated politically, economically, and socially by Anglo-Americans to being one controlled by Mexican American politicians. With the influx of federal monies and federal and state agency jobs, Mexican Americans were able to offset somewhat the Anglo-American economic hold on the town.

Today, Robstown is a community with divisive political campaigns but few ideological or racial polarizations. Two of its native sons have become the most powerful politicians in the county by occupying the district's congressional seat and the county judgeship. Although life has not changed drastically for all the poor in the town, they now have a myriad of federal and state programs to attend to many of their needs. More important, the school system has more Mexican American administrators and teachers to look after the needs of its Chicano student population, and more graduates are attending the region's universities and colleges. Students also do not face the blatant racism of the past in the classroom.

The Movement did not solve the majority of problems in Robstown. Economically, Familias Unidas did not bring new jobs, attract new industry, or provide job training. Housing did not improve because of the group's activism. The quality of politicians improved only slightly. Robstown still faces a brain drain, as its young people leave to find opportunities elsewhere. And many Mexican American youth still face problems of identity and feel inferior to their Anglo-American counterparts.[45] Many are still ill-prepared to attend college, and the school board has done little to establish a Chicano studies curriculum.[46] There is also a growing gang problem in the community, and violence remains a constant in this small town where almost everyone owns a weapon. The Movement also could not stop the decline of the town. American rural communities have been declining since the mid-century. No social movement can stop this and, in fact, may accelerate the process as young people see the futility of remaining in communities where many opportunities are connected to familial networks and where there are few resources to accomplish significant changes in the society.

The Movement in Robstown, however, accomplished more than it did in other areas, given the Movement's own limitations. The Movement brought the one-person, one-vote, majority-rule concept to Robstown. Voting has become an exercise for all residents rather than just for the middle and lower middle class. With the agitation and the electoral challenges of Familias Unidas, most old-time Anglo-American politicians who had been elected by a small minority were swept out of office. The style of politics has also changed. Before, Mexican Americans running for office had to be cautious not to offend the Anglo-American community; now they run as *hijos del pueblo* (sons or daughters of the people), with pledges to work for the Mexican American majority. Politics in Robstown are now carried on among Mexican American families, oftentimes within the confines of the barrio, and no longer in private offices. The Movement also helped Robstown's Mexican American officials become part of the overall effort by Mexican Americans to find their niche in Texan society. Robstown politicians are now part of the statewide group of Mexican American elected officials seeking to speak with a collective "Hispanic" voice on behalf of the *comunidad*.[47] This, in some ways, makes them slightly more liberal and forward looking than if they had remained trapped in solely small-town politics. In fact, on the state level, these politicians participate in much more liberal circles, and their politics are closer to those of Chicano activists than those of their predecessors.

Through the challenge of activists, many of the jobs in the school district and the city government have now gone to Mexican American natives of Robstown. This is an important change, because these jobs are some of the most prized in a community with a limited industrial base. Although the jobs are not high paying, they are stable and less physically demanding than others. They provide benefits and retirement pensions. For Mexican Americans seeking to stay in Robstown, these jobs are as good as it gets. Upward mobility for Mexican Americans has become a reality because many more are educated and can assume professional positions. Also, familial networks work to keep putting Chicanos into the system, whether it be in the city government or the school district.

The Movement process clearly played itself out in Robstown. The rejection of the liberal agenda proved much more defined in this community than in Crystal City, where clearly the battle was between Anglo-Americans and Chicanos. In Robstown, the struggle pitted Chicano activists and their supporters against the Anglo and Mexican American coalitions that dominated the town's politics. Chicanos were asked to choose between old-line Anglo politics and Mexican American accommodation and a Chicano nationalist political line. In Robstown, the polarization went beyond Anglo-American on one side and Mexican American on the other. When Chicano activists lambasted and criticized Mexican American politicians, they were not only branding them *vendidos,* they were rejecting their profoundly held beliefs of what was good for Mexican Americans. These beliefs were rooted in the liberal politics of the Mexican American Generation.

The Chicano reinterpretation of history proved more subtle in Robstown, because the activists there were at times anti-intellectual and much more constrained by barrio militancy. They tended to engage less in intellectual discussions about internal colonialism or Chicano nationalism than did their counterparts in other areas. Nonetheless, Chicano activists and their supporters did interpret their own experiences as one of struggle against gringo oppression and Mexican American *vendidismo.* They looked to the older members of the families as survivors of Anglo-American discrimination. In their minds, the Robstown community had not been a conglomeration of unskilled, marginalized laborers, but rather a community of hard-working people with an internal life and a tenacity for survival. Chicano activists continually emphasized the organic intellectualism of La Raza. They taught that the community had always had the ability to pull itself out of its economic and social dilemmas but had been prevented from doing so by Anglo-American racism.

In terms of class and racial definition, Robstown activists were able to differentiate *la gente* from the Mexican American middle class and its accommodationist politics. Middle-class leaders saw themselves as spokespersons and negotiators for La Raza. They represented the individualism of American society. Familias Unidas, in contrast, served as a vehicle for joining powerless Mexican Americans into a whole that gave them power through numbers and sheer organizational tenacity. Familias Unidas members became proud of their background, barrios, food, language, and new sense of liberation. They became "Corky" Gonzales's *raza de bronce* by defining themselves as *los de abajo* (the underdogs) on the way up. By engaging in politics, Chicanos in Robstown empowered themselves emotionally even while remaining powerless as individuals. The personification of La Raza reaffirmed their *chicanismo*.

By debating and discussing issues, Mexican Americans learned to comprehend power relations. By strategizing and executing their plans, they learned to be political. And by winning elections, they learned the concept of empowerment. This was their politics of Aztlán. They became empowered by defining the enemy, attacking its power base, and seeking to change the style and substance of political leadership. As they struggled for control of the community, they became active participants in the larger community. They were no longer just complainers and protesters. Their collective person had become political. What occurred in Robstown occurred in a number of South Texas communities with different rates of success. But collectively the individual processes came to form one major Chicano Movement process.

CHAPTER SIX

The Ethos and Its Legacy

The Chicano Movement, in its most basic form, represented a profound questioning of the Chicano experience in American society and a yearning for the politics of self-determination. Its primary goal was not simply finding an identity, as some have argued, but rather liberating Mexican Americans from racism, poverty, political powerlessness, historical neglect, and internal defeatism. Identity became important to the process, but so did the development of progressive politics. Movement activists supported the struggles of all peoples of color, savagely attacked racism, and oriented Chicanos toward compassion for the poor, the imprisoned, the abused, and even the misguided criminal element. It rhetorically and emotionally—if not always in practice—rejected welfare capitalism and its demeaning nature. It denounced imperialism, both capitalist and socialist, and it saw through the condescension of much of the liberalism of the times. And most of all it promoted cultural nationalism, because Mexican Americans continued to find themselves outside the American mainstream.

The Movement ethos encompassed ideas on the nature of Chicano oppression and highlighted resistance to that oppression. The ethos, notwithstanding its working-class base, reflected middle-class reformism and various leftist ideologies. The involvement of students and their liberal lifestyles accentuated the American strains within the loose ideology.[1] This ethos spread out from the regions where Movement activities were present. Although each Chicano group or organization borrowed heavily from the others, each remained preoccupied with its own activities and its own societal backlash. Cohesion and commonality came from the shared experiences that affected most Chicanos in most places. Because the Movement proved to be as much a process as an event, or series of events, its influence permeated even those areas where there were no major Chicano organizations. The rejection of the liberal agenda, the reinterpretation of history, the affirmation of class and race, and the politics of opposition were strategies that, in their purest forms, did not require major militant organizations or established leaders to occur.

In developing a militant ethos, Chicanos deviated from the politics of the past. They no longer desired to return to Mexico, as did the earlier Mexican immigrants, nor did they seek simply to integrate into American society, as did the Mexican American Generation. Chicano activists, *políticos,* and intellectuals argued for a polity that explained their historical presence in American society and yet differentiated them from Anglo-Americans. They wanted an ideology that accepted them as they were yet gave them the impetus to take their place among the people of the world. This yearning expressed itself through the founding of organizations. This was logical, since Mexican Americans saw themselves as individually powerless. Historically, Mexican Americans had come together at different times to confront their problems. Although individualism remained important, it tended to be individualism within an organization. For the working class, the concept of the *pueblo* was of utmost importance. This collectivism helped to tie them to Mexican history, a history most saw as heroic.

A number of scholars have argued that students and young people were the main catalysts of the Movement. Judging from the number of young people involved, and the number of youth organizations founded, this seems true on the surface. But a closer look at the Movement reveals that it remained dominated not by students or youth but by adults who had experienced Anglo-American prejudice for an extended period. Of the four principal leaders of the Movement—César Chávez, Reies López Tijerina, José Angel Gutiérrez, and Rodolfo "Corky" Gonzales—only Gutiérrez was in his twenties and a student when he became a leader in the Movement. Other leaders such as Bert Corona, Dolores Huerta, Virginia Múzquiz, Raul Ruiz, Mario Compean, and countless others were beyond their mid-twenties, an age at which Mexican Americans are no longer considered young.

In American society, the university has extended youth past the mid-twenties. But in a community where most of its young adult population does not attend college and is working at an early age, the twenties signify adulthood. To argue that Chicano activists were predominantly youthful is to misunderstand cultural characteristics of the Mexican American community. The "youthful" activists were at an age when most of their peers were already working and taking care of families. This does not deny their youthful characteristics, but it should be pointed out that the successful organizations were those that tended to work with adults and that were not university based. The reason is obvious. While scholars at the universities philosophically explored the limitations of the Mexican American community, and the difference between it and that of Anglo-Americans, the real impact of this difference was experienced in the barrio. There, adults lived in a permanent environment that required more than an office of Chicano student affairs, or representation on faculty and student committees, to make fundamental changes. Most youth in the Movement were involved not as students but as Chicanos. Some were influenced by the New Left and Black Power movements, but the most influential activists were those who agitated within their barrios rather than at the university. Many of the scholars who have written about the Movement were influenced by student-oriented politics. Thus, their conclusions are affected by their experiences. The reality of the Movement was not a large number of young people—or students—"raising Cain," but one of a community struggling to survive and to control its destiny. Movement activities only became legitimate when older people and whole families supported them. Only when the elders of the community responded and created a generational link did the Movement have an impact. To see the Movement as strictly or predominantly a student or youth affair is to limit its impact on the community. Chicano youth formed the vanguard of the Movement, but the collective experience of Chicanos proved its dominant inspiration. The main leaders of the Movement were those who transcended the Chicano generation back historically and bound their present struggle to those of the past.

When Chicano activists rejected the liberal agenda, they called into question the status of all Chicanos in the United States who had been marginalized by the politics of that agenda. This rejection placed Mexican Americans outside the political mainstream, removing Movement participants from the mass of forgotten people and converting them into advocates for their barrios. In rejecting Anglo-American leaders and their barrio cronies, the Movement created an aperture for organic leaders and groups. The rejection called into question the supremacy of the American political and economic system, thus allowing Chicano intellectuals to regain a role in the pursuit of options for the Mexican American community. Unlike the participants of the civil-rights movement who still believed in a fundamentally just America, many in the Chicano Movement questioned whether Mexican Americans could ever receive justice. For a people without a version of American history, this rejection was key to eliminating the sense of inferiority prevalent among many in the barrio.

Rejection loosened a generation's creative and intellectual bonds. In doing so, Chicanos began the process of reinterpreting their history and further removing themselves from the constraints of historical and intellectual marginalization. History, often used as a weapon to oppress Mexican Americans, became the main catalyst for freeing them. Their historical interpretation was not constrained by the university but rather enhanced by Chicanos within it. This interpretation proved to be an ongoing interpretation. Chicano history, Chicano sociology, Chicano psychology, and a host of other social science paradisciplines came into existence. With these new paradisciplines, Anglo-Americans ceased to be the interpreters of the Chicano experience, or its legitimizers. Concentrating on class and race as determinants of commitment to the Movimiento, the Movement became grounded in the working class, where the majority of Mexican Americans remained. Cultural legitimacy came to depend on the Chicano *volk*. Chicano arts and letters shunned much of the radical and mainstream art of the 1960s and 1970s and concentrated on depicting Mexican American daily life, and Chicano and Mexican heroism.

In seeking new interpretations, the Movement created an opening for Chicanas to affirm their own identity within the community. Chicanas fought against traditional gender roles within the Chicano family by taking positions of leadership, walking the picket lines, getting arrested, and running as candidates on independent Chicano slates. But they also sought to bridge the gap between the public life of activism and the private life of the family. They did so through feminist discussions of family roles and by strengthening their role within the Movement. Chicana activists came to view the oppression of women in the barrio as threefold: they were female, of color, and poor. This meant that Chicana activists had to enlarge the political agenda from one concerned with race and national origins to one that included gender and familial roles. Chicana activists forced male activists to change their rhetoric and slowly become more inclusive of women's issues. They also created a political paradigm that made the discussion of Chicana issues a permanent part—theoretically if not always in practice—of the polemics of the struggle for self-determination.

Chicana feminists took two approaches.[2] One was to work outside, or on the periphery, of the male-dominated organizations and maintain a watchdog attitude against *machismo*. Those who took this approach were the women who conducted and refined feminist thought among Chicanas. They were also the ones who created alliances with white women and attempted to sensitize the overall women's movement to the plight of Chicanas. The other approach kept Chicanas close to the core of Chicano activism. These women served in roles opened to them and, through their organizational skills and value to particular groups, rose in the male hierarchy. Although less active in the creation of Chicana feminist thought, they were able to force the Movement organizations to include women's issues in the platforms, conference agendas, and ideological discussions of the Chicano experience. The majority of Chicanas within the Movement were not feminist per se; they participated simply because they believed in *la causa*. But their participation was the beginning of the process of injecting or reinjecting women into the role of public leader within their communities. This entrance into the public arena was one of the main accomplishments of the Chicano Movement. From then on, Chicanas became a part of the Chicano electoral core.[3]

The Movement did not alienate Chicanas in general, as some scholars have argued. What the nationalist movement did was to attempt to define the role of Chicanas within a context that was nationalist. Women were not to be subservient as they had been defined earlier, but neither were they to be completely divorced from the community as some radical white feminists sought. The activists, both male and female, sought to converge the role of the nurturer with that of the *soldadera*. But rather than the role of a superwoman, Chicano and Chicana activists wanted one that came closest to achieving a balance. In fact, their efforts were an attempt to legitimize a role already assumed by many women in the Movement and in the barrio. They could point to Dolores Huerta, Virginia Múzquiz, Luz Gutiérrez, Rosie

Castro, Lupe Castillo, Enriqueta Longeaux y Vásquez, and other women who succeeded in assuming the new role. Unfortunately for Chicano activists, their inability to gain control of their communities limited the opportunities to put into practice their own version of women's liberation. Crystal City proved one of the few laboratories for the new strategies. In the political and electoral arena, a number of women there were able to blossom and become an integral part of the power elite.[4] They headed the main organizations, were elected to city and county offices, and participated in most of the activities of La Raza Unida Party. But since La Raza Unida Party never did succeed in gaining significant economic patronage in Crystal City, women did not reach economic parity with the men. Most of the bureaucratic and educational jobs went to men from outside the community who had the education and training needed to run the "revolution." Some believe that Chicana integration would have occurred if the party had been able to control the town's economic sector. This conjecture does not deny the dynamics of male/female relations. There were still significant conflicts between the women and the men in the party. Women's roles were still restricted by the community's social mores. But the women leaders with political office and large numbers of women supporters were negotiating with strength. The *cristalinas* had learned to play political hardball.

The Movement's effect on Chicanas can best be appreciated when one considers that the Movement lasted so short a time and yet produced so many women leaders and intellectuals. One reason that the literature on Chicanas in the Movement has been scarce is the fact that most Chicana nationalists pursued interests other than academic ones, whereas Chicana non-nationalists went into the universities and have since written most of the literature. Chicana nationalists were women who saw as their role models the Mexican *revolucionarias* such as Juana Gallo, La Valentina, La Corregidora, and others. They also admired the socialist women of Cuba and North Vietnam, and the *guerrilleras* of other Third World countries who remained committed to their overall struggles and did not separate themselves by gender. This is not to say that they were better than those who did organize themselves based on gender. It is rather an observation that is meant to rescue many Chicana nationalists from the ideological graveyard and from the ranks of the "political groupies." After seeing Maria Elena Martínez, Lucy González, Viviana Santiago, Rosie Castro, and Martha Cotera in action, and hearing about Lupe Castillo, Cecilia Baldenegro, and others, it is hard to imagine them as manipulated women or political groupies. They accomplished too much, fought too hard, and influenced too many to be disregarded in the literature on the Movement. Many are still active today, and a number are involved in women's issues; most still point to the Chicano Movement as their training ground.

The Movement's strategies for political empowerment had the greatest impact on the creation of a militant ethos. Electoral campaigns, protest marches, grassroots organizing, boycotts, and activist training all produced a political paradigm that saw the Chicano community as an entity dependent on itself and not outsiders. Chicanos became the creators of political agendas, educational curriculums, and new artistic fashions. Chicano activists and elected officials came to look at Mexican American constituencies as permanent, on whom they could depend for their political future. A community with leaders and supporters provided a sense of peoplehood. This new definition gave Mexican Americans an identity and placed an obligation on them to determine their own future.

The sense of peoplehood, however, never subsumed the inherent contradictions of the political parts. In Kingsville the poem *Yo Soy Joaquín* and the manifesto the Plan Espiritual de Aztlán were used for recruiting purposes and in the hours-long indoctrination sessions. Yet we were *gutierristas* and saw the author of these two works, Gonzales of the Crusade for Justice, as the one who had split the Movement through his constant criticism of La Raza Unida Party in Texas.[5] In our La Raza Unida Club, we had students who belonged to different factions, including the Barrio Club, a group that competed directly with Gutiérrez's Ciudadanos Unidos for control of the city and county governments. Our explanation to those who thought it strange emphasized the organizing efforts of Kingsville over external alliances or conflicts. The failure to establish a significant national structure forced Chicano groups such as the one in Kingsville to see all issues in a regional context before they saw them in a national light. As activists we realized that most working-class Chicanos were concerned with local issues. Although many may have been interested in national issues, few mechanisms existed for the majority of Movimiento supporters to participate beyond their localities.

During the Bakke case in 1976, which dealt with reverse discrimination in the University of California's medical school,[6] the Kingsville group invited Juan Gómez-Quiñones and Antonio Rodríguez to speak on campus. Gómez-Quiñones was disliked by a number of the Kingsville activists for his critique of cultural nationalism. And Rodríguez headed CASA. Yet the Bakke case represented a crucial battleground in the fight over accessibility to higher education. Seeking to be part of the national debate on affirmative action and hoping to reignite the waning political passions of the barrio, we created an "event" around their visit. Introducing them as "a Chicano scholar and Chicano-rights lawyer," we used their presence to maintain our visibility in the community at large and at the university. After their visit, we continued to use their propaganda to promote our own battle with the university administration. The arguments against Bakke, and those against our own university administration, came out of the pool of political ideas that had arisen during the Movement. Consequently, we could share the rhetoric and propaganda of an "adversary" for our own purposes without betraying our political integrity or revealing the contradictions within the larger Movement.

In Kingsville, our political culture evolved through the four-step process. We rejected Anglo-American politicians, academicians, and their ideas. And we saw the past political strategies of middle-class Mexican Americans as accommodationist failures. We interpreted the history of our region as one of struggle between poor, rural *mexicanos*, and the King Ranch, Texas Rangers, political bosses, and Mexican American *vendidos*. Our regional history was the history of Rodolfo Acuña's *Occupied America* and Gonzales's *Yo Soy Joaquín*. We marginalized the influential middle class of South Texas and Kingsville philosophically and culturally by indoctrinating students and community people to the "superiority" of the working class. Although middle-class Mexican Americans continued to dominate the electoral politics of the barrio, they often came to us for ideas and rhetoric in their campaigns against Anglo-American politicians. Even after we began competing in the electoral arena, they attempted to maintain a friendly relationship because they felt ideologically weak and needed some of our rhetoric. In other areas the relationships were less accommodating. Nonetheless, Mexican American reformers took possession of much of the rhetoric of the Movement, though with a softer tone and a less conflictive posture.

Our politics, often contradictory organizationally because we depended heavily on students and academic professionals, were the politics of opposition. We engaged in oppositional rhetoric, giving practical meaning and application to concepts such as self-determination, liberation, *chicanismo,* and *concientización,* even though we could explain most of these concepts only in the abstract. We understood their meaning only within the context of a political ethos that saw us as working-class Chicanos struggling against political, social, and cultural oppression. Only through that historical construct could we be as scathingly critical of American society as we were back then. Failure to reinterpret our history through a nationalist paradigm meant we had to accept that things were better than before and that some Chicanos were benefiting from American capitalism. Years later, a number of Chicano leaders still had trouble defining some of the terms they themselves had repeated so often. Said one Chicana leader in 1986, "I never really understood what we meant by 'self-determination.' Was it revolution, or a nation within a nation?"[7]

Our political strategies and our tactics were very much within the context of the feminist Chela Sandoval's differential opposition.[8] We did politically what worked for us. Because our *chicanismo* reflected our rhetoric and our abstract ideas, we could rationalize ideological consistency. The hodgepodge of ideas and cultural symbols represented a reservoir of political catch phrases, and their application as strategies homogenized them into an ethos. Once the process began and matured at varying speeds in the different regions, it replaced the politics of the Mexican American Generation, or in some places, the traditional barrio accommodationist politics. With time, even more moderate organizations that succeeded the Movement, such as the Mexican American Democrats, retained many aspects of the ethos, even while avoiding the politics of confrontation. This ethos never acquired the rigid structure of an ideology, but it did serve to give Mexican Americans a sense of political identity by providing nationalist rhetoric, ideas, strategies, electoral platforms, and political victories. All of these added to the reservoir of ideas and catch phrases that made Chicano political dialogue possible.

The Chicano Movement, like other movements of Mexican Americans, declined because it reached the limits of its applicability, notwithstanding its failure to achieve its stated goals. Self-determination, liberation, Brown Power, Aztlán, and other similar rhetorical concepts served as catalysts for political action but represented a direct challenge to integrationist tendencies in American politics. Those concepts were foreign terms and had no translatable application to the American political system. By this I mean that these terms had not been used in traditional American political debates before. These terms raised questions about race and class conflicts and loyalty to the United States, and they challenged traditional polemics on American ideology. These terms came from Third World and socialist revolutionaries as well as from Mexican radicals of the past. When Mexican Americans began to enter the American mainstream through the apertures created by the Movement, they abandoned the Chicano Movement organizations that remained separatist in orientation. In the end, many Mexican Americans wanted "in" to the American mainstream. Their association with Chicano militant groups had been a reaction to the lack of accessibility to that mainstream. Chicano militants were never quite able to truly convert the majority of their followers to the fundamentals of *chicanismo*. For those who did not "learn" the new history, or did not engage in philosophical marathons, the opening of American society was the end result of activism. As Chicano activists were moving away from American society, many Mexican Americans were moving toward the small openings in it.

The aperture was class specific. Middle-class Mexican Americans, and those on the rise to the middle class, saw new opportunities in federal and state jobs and in a private sector more aware of the potential "Hispanic" market. For those who had little education, lacked citizenship, or clung to their nationalism, the openings were limited. Mexican Americans who could moved toward a less hostile Anglo-American mainstream that rewarded accommodation and integration. This move appears logical if Mexican American history is seen as a progressive battle for self-determination. Chicanos abandon one strategy and embrace another as a way to continue solving the problems of the barrios.[9] This again is consistent with Sandoval's "differential opposition."

I do not want to downplay the external forces that led to the Movement's decline. From judicial litigations to espionage and infiltration, subversive tactics were used against Movement organizations and individuals involved in activism. The onslaught was constant and intense.[10] People lost jobs, were arrested, suffered economic hardships, and became socially marginalized in their community because of their activism. The constant pressure on activists also led to internal conflicts. While the Movement grew quickly, conflict was less apparent. Victory against the gringo united the different groups. But as political victories became more difficult and activists had to solidify organization goals, conflicts arose. *Personalismo* became common as individual leaders sought to retain or expand their position within the Movement. With the infiltration of more radical leftist ideas, a split occurred between the nationalists and the leftists, and then within the groups themselves. The lack of a national structure, a dominant leader, and an explicit ideology made it impossible to retain solidarity among such diverse groups. But the most devastating *internal* blow was the inability of Chicano organizations to participate in the political openings they had created. Their own politics of separatism, and the mainstream's disdain of them, opened doors for more-moderate Chicanos, using some of the same rhetoric, to replace the Movement activists as the new power brokers in the barrio.

The Chicano Movement's lashing out at the "system" or the *gringo* occurred alongside a more traditional civil-rights effort by more-moderate Mexican American reformers.[11] These reformers never lost their faith in American institutions. They first emulated the efforts of the black civil-rights movement and then became more ethnically conscious and more militant. The Chicano activists and moderate reformers meshed at different times and complemented each other. Eventually they came to be in opposition. Chicano militants moved away from the moderate Mexican Americans, but the Chicano reinterpretation of history and its promotion of working-class history and barrio culture pulled the moderate groups toward a more nationalistic stance. Many moderate reformers followed the Movement part of the way. This allowed them to break from the traditional liberal agenda and turn to what historian Mario T. García calls postliberalism. This postliberalism accepts the status of ethnicity, promotes bilingualism as a right, recognizes the historical divergence of the Chicano experience, and is sensitive to the needs of poor Mexican Americans and to the dilemmas of the undocumented worker.[12] With the demise of the Movement, the "old" Mexican Americans, the Chicanos, and the new recruits to reform and activism joined to form what I call the Mexican American/Hispanic Generation.

This generation is a hybrid of the two preceding ones, encompassing ideals of both.[13] This new generation of Mexican American leaders, while moving away from much of the separatist politics of Aztlán, retains much of the former militants' agenda. This agenda seeks a strong ethnic identity and a politics of empowerment, rather than just integration. Few Mexican Americans can run for political office or seek leadership in the community without promoting themselves as being part of the *comunidad*. As political or community leaders, they belong to ethnic-specific organizations and speak "for" Mexican Americans as a whole. Their importance outside their individual political districts lies in the fact that they are spokespersons for the community. The unity among them is based as much on ethnic-oriented issues as on personal ideology. The politics of Aztlán, which replaced the politics of status, have now been replaced by the politics of ethnicity, but many of the concerns remain the same.[14] Activists are still concerned about educational accessibility, poor housing, discrimination in employment, police brutality, media stereotypes, undocumented immigration, and cultural identity.

Much like the Mexican Revolution in Mexico, *chicanismo* has been institutionalized into the political mainstream of the Mexican American community, albeit with some significant variations. Mexican American Hispanics do not promote separatism, Aztlán, or confrontation. They do not speak as openly about Anglo-American racism and are less likely to promote themselves as the "Chicano" candidate to the general populace. Consequently, in the same manner that the institutionalization of the Mexican Revolution destroyed its passion, moderated its rhetoric, and created its elite structure, so has the institutionalization of the Chicano ethos. Mexican American leaders, however, do remain skeptical of traditional liberal agendas and interpret their experiences from an ethnic point of view, and Chicano art, Chicano literature, and Chicano music remain a product of the Movement. In the absence of a strong Hispanic academic presence, Chicano scholars remain the intellectuals of the Mexican American community, though they play a smaller part in the community's activist dialogue than they did during the Movement. Within the larger liberal coalitions of which Mexican American Hispanics are a part, ethnic aspirations must be kept to an acceptable level—acceptable to the liberal, pluralistic mainstream. Needless to say, profound discussions of what it means to be a Chicano are no longer a public affair outside of esoteric academic journals and monographs with limited circulation.

Chicano activists would argue that Mexican American Hispanics have abandoned the Chicano ethos for a return to integration and that their coalitions with Anglo-American politicians represent an abandonment of self-determination. But they would be only partly correct. Mexican American Hispanics simply face the same pressures to integrate that preceding generations of Mexican Americans in the twentieth century have had to deal with. Their response, which is yet to be interpreted fully, will be another effort at the interpretation of history, and an accommodation or reaction to the existing politics. The difference may be that this generation now praises a new class—professional activists, politicians, and bureaucrats—and receives only marginal input from the working class.[15]

The legacy of the Chicano Movement lies not so much in what it accomplished but in the way Mexican American political thought changed. The Movement institutionalized a political counterculture that defines itself through its ethnicity and historical experience. Mexican American politicians now depend on this counterculture to maintain their identity and their political leadership. In a sense they promote political integration concurrently with their promotion of ethnicity. This is a variation of the Chicano activists' promotion of civil rights even as they promoted cultural separatism. In promoting this dichotomy, Mexican American Hispanics keep the Chicano Movement's goals of self-determination and cultural solidarity alive—if only barely, in the minds of former Movement activists. In this they are assisted by the continuing resistance of Anglo-America. The strategies of the Movement may well disappear at the turn of the century, but its legacy will live on.

Notes

INTRODUCTION

1. The two best works describing Chicano resistance to Anglo-American domination are Rodolfo Acuña's *Occupied America: The Chicano Struggle for Liberation* (San Francisco: Canfield Press, 1972); and Robert J. Rosenbaum's *Mexicano Resistance in the Southwest: The Sacred Right of Self-Preservation* (Austin: University of Texas Press, 1981).

2. This militant ethos has been described as *"chicanismo."* See Carlos Muñoz, *Youth, Identity, Power* (London: Verso, 1989); and Juan Gómez-Quiñones, *Chicano Politics: Reality and Promise, 1940–1990* (Albuquerque: University of New Mexico Press, 1990).

3. Carlos Muñoz argues in his book that the Chicano Movement was a struggle over identity; see *Youth, Identity, Power,* 8–12. Gómez-Quiñones calls it the "politics of identity"; see *Chicano Politics,* 102–5.

4. The internal-colony model posited that Mexican Americans were a conquered people subjected to the conditions of a colonial society: discrimination, a dual wage system, the cooptation of its elites, and ruthless violence.

5. By his second edition, Acuña had changed his mind and used the model for only the nineteenth century. In his third edition, he downplays the model almost to its exclusion. See Acuña, *Occupied America: A History of Chicanos,* 3d ed. (New York: Harper & Row, 1988).

6. Acuña, *Occupied America,* 3d ed., 1–5.

7. Mario Barrera, *Beyond Aztlán: Ethnic Autonomy in Comparative Perspective* (New York: Praeger, 1988), 44.

8. Ibid., 33–44.

9. Gómez-Quiñones, *Chicano Politics,* 101.

10. Ibid., 103.

11. Ibid.

12. Ibid., 104.

13. For further discussion, see Gómez-Quiñones, *Mexican Students por la Raza: The Chicano Student Movement in Southern California, 1967–1977* (Santa Barbara, Calif.: Editorial La Causa, 1978).

14. Muñoz, *Youth, Identity, Power,* 15–16.

15. Ibid., 16.

16. For a discussion of the growing middle-class militancy of the 1960s, see Robert A. Cuellar, "A Social and Political History of the Mexican American Population of Texas, 1929–1963" (master's thesis, Texas State University, Denton, 1969). Also see Gómez-Quiñones, *Chicano Politics,* 88–97.

17. Much literature was written during the Movement years on the meaning of being Chicano or Chicana. Even the origins of the word "Chicano" were debated and discussed continually. See Bob Morales, "Chicano: Word Symbol of Confusion or Cohesion?" *Coraje* 1, no. 2 (April 1969): 8; see also Guillermo Fuenfrios, "The Emergence of the New Chicano," in *Aztlán: An Anthology of Mexican American Literature,* ed. Luis Valdez and Stan Steiner (New York: Alfred A. Knopf, 1972), 283–88.

18. I use the term "peoplehood" because Chicanos never quite defined themselves as a nation, notwithstanding "El Plan Espiritual de Aztlán" (see chapter 4 for a discussion of this document).

19. Aztlán was the name of the legendary home of the Aztecs. Chicanos adopted that name to refer to the Southwest and their political utopia. See Luis Valdez's "La Plebe" in *Aztlán: An Anthology of Mexican American Literature,* ed. Luis Valdez and Stan Steiner (New York: Alfred A. Knopf, 1972), xxxi–xxxiv.

20. I would qualify this statement by saying that those who know the history have learned it at the university from Chicano historians.

CHAPTER 1

1. Mario T. García, *Mexican Americans: Leadership, Ideology and Identity, 1930–1960* (New Haven, Conn.: Yale University Press, 1989), 30.

2. Ibid., 31.

3. Alonso Perales and M. C. González were members of LULAC and were two of the most influential members of the Mexican American Generation. See M. T. García, *Mexican Americans,* and Richard García, *Rise of the Mexican American Middle Class: San Antonio, 1929–1941* (College Station: Texas A & M Press, 1991), for more on their activities.

4. For a discussion of early unionist activity by Mexican Americans in Texas, see Emilio Zamora, *The World of the Mexican Worker in Texas* (College Station: Texas A & M Press, 1993). This work has an extensive discussion of Mexicanist philosophy among activists of the early twentieth century. For early unionist activity in the Midwest, see Dennis Nodín Valdés, *Al Norte: Agricultural Workers in the Great Lakes Region, 1917–1970* (Austin: University of Texas Press, 1991), 31–50. For a good per-

spective on leftist and socialist politics among Mexican Americans at the turn of the century, see Juan Gómez-Quiñones, *Roots of Chicano Politics, 1600–1940* (Albuquerque: University of New Mexico Press, 1994), 342–51.

5. See the following works by Christine Marín: *La Asociación Hispano-Americana de Madres y Esposas: Tucson's Mexican American Women in World War II,* Renato Rosaldo Lecture Series Monograph 1 (Tucson: Mexican American Studies and Research Center, University of Arizona, 1985), 5–18; and "Mexican Americans on the Home Front: Community Organizations in Arizona during World War II," *Perspectives in Mexican American Studies* 4 (1993): 75–92. See also Richard Santillán, "Rosita the Riveter," *Perspectives in Mexican American Studies* 3 (1992).

6. For a discussion of Mexican American soldiers in World War II, see Raul Morín, *Among the Valiant: Mexican Americans in World War II and Korea* (Los Angeles: Borden, 1963). For their reaction to discrimination on their return from the war, see Carl Allsup, *The American G.I. Forum: Origins and Evolution* (Austin: University of Texas Press, 1982); and Alonso S. Perales, *The Mexican American: Are We Good Neighbors?* (New York: Arno Press, 1974).

7. See Abraham Hoffman, *Unwanted Mexican Americans in the Great Depression: Repatriation Pressures* (Tucson: University of Arizona Press, 1974); Juan Ramón García, *Operation Wetback: The Mass Deportation of Mexican Undocumented Workers in 1954* (Westport, Conn.: Greenwood Press, 1980); and Mark Reisler, *By the Sweat of Their Brow: Mexican Immigrant Labor in the United States* (Westport, Conn.: Greenwood Press, 1976).

8. For a discussion of the litigation battles, see M. T. García, *Mexican Americans,* 50–51. For a good history of the educational struggles in Texas, see Guadalupe San Miguel, *Let All of Them Take Heed* (Austin: University of Texas Press, 1987).

9. M. T. García, *Mexican Americans,* 111–41.

10. Ibid., chapters 6, 7, and 8.

11. M. T. García, *Mexican Americans,* 227.

12. Ibid., 222.

13. Ibid., 59; see also Cuellar, "Social and Political History."

14. Ed Idar, Jr., phone interview with author, San Antonio, Tex., February 26, 1996. Idar was a leader of the American G.I. Forum and its newsletter editor for a number of years.

15. "Forumeers Aid Kennedy Ride into Presidency on Mexican Burro," *News Bulletin,* November–December 1960.

16. "Viva Kennedy Clubs Deliver Biggest Texas Demo Gains," *The Press,* November 9, 1960, p. 1.

17. "Viva Kennedy Leaders in Revolt," *Valley Morning Star,* June 28, 1961.

18. "Battle Boils over Latin American as U.S. Judge," *Corpus Christi Caller,* January 14, 1961.

19. "Political Interests of Latins United," *Texas Observer* (September 15, 1961).

20. For the best work to date on PASSO, see Cuellar, "Social and Political History," chapters 5 and 6; see also Ronnie Dugger, "The Struggle for P.A.S.O.," *Texas Observer* (June 14, 1963): 3–6.

21. José Angel Gutiérrez, interview with author, Houston, Tex., May 24, 1988. See Cuellar, "Social and Political History," 55–62; Julian Samora and Joe Bernal, *Gunpowder Justice: A Reassessment of the Texas Rangers* (Notre Dame, Ind.: University of Notre Dame Press, 1979), 110–14; and John Staples Shockley, *Chicano Revolt in a Texas Town* (Notre Dame, Ind.: University of Notre Dame Press, 1974), 24–41.

22. See Dugger, "Struggle for P.A.S.O.," 5–6.

23. See Shockley, *Chicano Revolt,* 24–110, for a discussion of the rise and demise of Los Cinco.

24. Ibid.

25. This is a term coined by Arturo Madrid, former head of the Hispanic University, to describe the token few Mexican Americans who are in positions of power or influence.

26. See Leo Gebler, Joan W. Moore, and Ralph C. Guzmán, *The Mexican American People* (New York: Free Press, 1970), 18–23.

27. See Ignacio M. García, *United We Win* (Tucson: Mexican American Studies and Resource Center, University of Arizona, 1989), 2–5; see also Elroy Bode's "Requiem for a WASP School," in *Chicano: The Beginnings of Bronze Power,* ed. Renato Rosaldo, Gustave L. Seligmann, and Robert A. Calvert (New York: William Morrow & Co., 1974) for a discussion of the changing nature of some southwestern schools.

28. Gebler, Moore, and Guzmán, *Mexican American People,* 18–23.

29. See I. M. García, *United We Win,* 5; see also James T. Patterson, *America's Struggle against Poverty, 1900–1985* (Cambridge: Harvard University Press, 1986), 115, for a discussion of the government's policy toward migrant workers.

30. George I. Sánchez, *Forgotten People* (Albuquerque: University of New Mexico Press, 1940), 97.

31. Even socialist-oriented activists like Bert Corona kept themselves within the mainstream and rarely attacked American liberal ideology. See Mario T. García, *Memories of Chicano History: The Life and Narrative of Bert Corona* (Berkeley: University of California Press, 1994).

32. Hector P. García, Corpus Christi, Tex., to Manuel Avila, Jr., Caracas, Venezuela, July 22, 1961, Hector P. García Papers, Special Collections, Texas A & M University, Corpus Christi.

33. Letter to Manuel Avila, Jr., September 18, 1961, Hector P. García Papers.

34. Ronnie Dugger, "San Antonio Liberalism: Piecing It Together," *Texas Observer* (May 27, 1966): 1–5.

35. Raul Morín, Monterey, Calif., to Bob Rodriguez, San José, Calif., November 30, 1963, Hector P. García Papers.

36. In his book *LULAC: The Evolution of a Mexican American Political Organization* (Austin: University of Texas Press, 1993), Benjamin Márquez argues that ac-

tivism among groups remains firm as long as the "incentive" to agitate remains stronger or more beneficial than the burden that activism carries with it. For many Mexican American middle-class reformers, the burden of activism had become bigger than the incentives to change things. This was so because the initial incentive—that is, to change their own situation—had basically become moot.

37. César Chávez, "The Organizer's Tale," in *Chicano: The Beginnings of Bronze Power,* ed. Renato Rosaldo, Gustave L. Seligmann, and Robert A. Calvert (New York: William Morrow & Co., 1974), 57–62.

38. José Angel Gutiérrez, interview with author, Independence, Ore., January 1985.

39. Octavio Romano, "The Historical and Intellectual Presence of Mexican Americans," *El Grito* 2, no. 2 (1969): 32–46.

40. These grape-boycott committees captured the imagination of many in the barrio as well as non–Mexican Americans. While I was in basic training in the army, I, along with other Chicano soldiers, would ask whether the grapes served were union grapes. If they were not, I would boycott them. For many of us, the boycotts were one of the first ways in which we became involved and also became conscious that we were a national minority.

41. Muñoz argues that the Chicano Movement was part of a worldwide rebellion of youth. See Muñoz, *Youth, Identity, Power,* 12.

42. Other unions for Mexicans and Mexican Americans had existed before, but none had used their ethnicity and cultural symbolism as effectively or had been as inspirational to nonunion members as the NFWA. Also, most other unions had been local, had promoted their "Mexicanness," and had used Spanish names for their organizations. The NFWA was meant to be a national union, it understood its role as a union for Mexican Americans and others who lived and planned to stay in the United States, and its name was in English. The NFWA recognized its historical role as an organization for Chicanos, even though it always claimed to be a union for all farmworkers. See Acuña, *Occupied America,* 3d. ed., 174–84, for a discussion of some of the union activity among farmworkers in the early part of the twentieth century.

43. See "Congreso for Land and Cultural Reform," *El Grito del Norte,* November 1973–January 1974, pp. 5–7; and Francis L. Swadesh, "The Alianza Movement: Catalyst for Social Change in New Mexico," in *Chicano: The Beginnings of Bronze Power,* ed. Renato Rosaldo, Gustave L. Seligmann, and Robert A. Calvert (New York: William Morrow & Co., 1974), 27–43.

44. Richard Gardner, *Grito! Reies Tijerina and the New Mexico Land Grant War of 1967* (Indianapolis: Bobbs-Merrill Co., 1970), 101.

45. Ibid., 31–47.

46. Ibid., 117–32.

47. Ibid., 1–8.

48. Ibid., 265–82.

49. The best work to date on Rodolfo "Corky" Gonzales is Christine Marín's *A*

Spokesman of the Mexican American Movement: Rodolfo "Corky" Gonzales and the Fight for Chicano Liberation, 1966–1972 (San Francisco: R & E Research Associates, 1977); see also I. M. García's *United We Win,* 91–116.

50. I. M. García, *United We Win,* 91–116.

51. Ibid., 91–103.

52. Rodolfo Gonzales, *I Am Joaquín/Yo Soy Joaquín* (New York: Bantam Books, 1972).

53. I. M. García, *United We Win,* 91–103.

54. American imperialist designs in Latin America date back to the war with Mexico and included military or subversive action in Nicaragua, Panama, Guatemala, and Chile.

55. Although many Chicano groups tempered their nationalism enough to form coalitions with other groups, the Crusade for Justice remained staunchly nationalistic and antagonistic to coalitions with white groups, no matter how progressive they claimed to be.

56. For a recent work on the Mexican American Youth Organization, see *Mexican American Youth Organization* (Austin: University of Texas Press, 1995) by Armando Navarro; see also I. M. García's *United We Win.*

57. Mario Compean, interview with author, Tucson, Ariz., September 10, 1985. Mario Compean was one of the founders of MAYO and La Raza Unida Party in Texas.

58. Armando Navarro, "El Partido de la Raza Unida in Crystal City: A Peaceful Revolution" (Ph.D. diss., University of California, Riverside, 1974), 557.

59. "On the History of LRUP," *Para la Gente* 1, no. 4 (October 1977): 13.

60. *Congressional Record,* April 15, 1969: 9059. See also an article by Kemper Diehl, "MAYO Leaders Warn of Violence, Rioting," *San Antonio Express and News* (reprinted in *Congressional Record,* April 3, 1969: 8591).

61. See Stephen Casanova, "The Movement for Bilingual/Bicultural Education in Texas: School Boycotts and the Mexican American Youth Organization," personal collection of I. M. García. Casanova was a close friend of most of the MAYO founders and leaders.

62. See the platform of La Raza Unida Party in I. M. García, *United We Win,* 83–85.

63. These quotations are taken from two undated letters found in the Ramsey Muñiz files in the Raza Unida Party Collection, Mexican American Archives, University of Texas, Austin.

64. Armando Rendón, *Chicano Manifesto: The History and Aspirations of the Second Largest Minority in America* (New York: Macmillan, 1971), 354.

65. Marcienne Rocard, *The Children of the Sun,* trans. Edmund G. Brown, Jr. (Tucson: University of Arizona Press, 1989), 255.

66. This quote is taken from a compilation of Corona's speeches: *Bert Corona Speaks on La Raza Unida Party and the Illegal Alien Scare* (New York: Pathfinder

Press, 1972), 8–9; for more on Corona, see Carlos Larralde, *Mexican American Movements and Leaders* (Los Alamitos, Calif.: Hwong, 1976), 168–83. For information on MAPA, see Miguel David Tirado, "Mexican American Community Political Organization," *Aztlan* 1 (1970): 53–78.

67. For more on this part of Corona's activities, see David Gutiérrez, *CASA in the Chicano Movement: Ideology and Organizational Politics in the Chicano Community 1968–1978,* Working Paper Series, no. 5 (Tucson: Mexican American Studies and Research Center, University of Arizona, 1984).

68. Galarza held a doctoral degree and was considered an important intellectual of the 1950s. He never held a position at a university, but his writings were used in the academy.

69. For a discussion of the La Raza Unida organization that preceded the political party of the same name, see I. M. García, *United We Win,* 20.

70. Mario Compean, interview with author, Boulder, Colo., April 14, 1988; see also I. M. García, *United We Win,* 19–20.

71. No significant work has been done on Ernesto Galarza except for a major exhibit on his work at the University of California at Los Angeles in the late 1980s. See Joan London and Henry Anderson, "Man of Fire: Ernesto Galarza," in *Chicano: The Beginnings of Bronze Power,* ed. Renato Rosaldo, Gustave L. Seligmann, and Robert A. Calvert (New York: William Morrow & Co., 1974), 38–52.

72. María Hernández was a community organizer since the 1940s, whereas Virginia Músquiz began her activism in the early 1960s. Although little has been written about them, Martha Cotera does include them in her book *Diosa y hembra* (Austin, Tex.: Information Systems Development, 1976).

73. Músquiz came to be known as Gutiérrez's mentor; and Hernández was one of the honored guests at the first La Raza Unida Party's state convention in 1972. See Cotera, *Diosa y hembra,* for more on them.

74. Letter to the Editor, *El Gallo,* November 15, 1967, p. 3.

75. This was a claim throughout the Chicano Movement period by activists who saw minimal involvement among Anglo-Americans in the barrio's struggle for equality.

76. I. M. García, *United We Win,* 108.

77. Ruben Bonilla represented a more militant force as president of LULAC during the late 1970s. He was the first LULAC president to meet with Chicano radicals and to use some of their rhetoric in attacking government inaction on Chicano concerns. Raul Yzaguirre also remained a close friend of some of the Chicano Movement leaders such as José Angel Gutiérrez.

CHAPTER 2

1. One who did was Carlos E. Castañeda, who wrote what historian Mario T. García calls a "complementary history" of the Mexican American. This history attempted

to underscore the similarities between Mexican Americans and Anglo-Americans. It also sought to dispel the stereotypes that Anglo-Americans had about Mexican Americans. For a further explanation of Castañeda's work, see Mario T. García, *In Search of History: Carlos E. Castañeda and the Mexican American Generation,* Renato Rosaldo Lecture Series Monograph 4 (Tucson: Mexican American Studies and Research Center, University of Arizona, 1988), 1–20.

2. John C. Hammerback, Richard J. Jensen, and José Angel Gutiérrez, *A War of Words* (Westport, Conn.: Greenwood Press, 1985), 51.

3. See the following works for an example of this type of scholarship: Celia S. Heller, *Mexican-American Youth: Forgotten Youth at the Crossroads* (New York: Random House, 1968); William Madsen, *Mexican-Americans of South Texas, Case Studies in Cultural Anthropology* (New York: Holt, Rinehart and Winston, 1964); Ruth Tuck, *Not with the Fist* (New York: Harcourt, Brace and Co., 1946); and Edmonson S. Munro, *Los Manitos: A Study of Institutional Values* (New Orleans: Middle American Research Institute, 1957).

4. "Poverty of culture" was developed as a concept from the writings of men like Oscar Lewis, Michael Harrington, and Daniel Moynihan. Ironically, all three authors claimed to write on behalf of the disadvantaged but ended up coining concepts that were used to blame the victims of poverty. See Oscar Lewis, *La Vida: A Puerto Rican Family in the Culture of Poverty* (New York: Random House, 1966); and Michael Harrington, *The New American Poverty* (New York: Penguin Books, 1984).

5. Valdez referred to the Spanish Conquest of Mexico, but other activists would use the term "conquest" to describe the occupation of the American Southwest by the U.S. military, which is what it refers to here. Whereas Anglo-American scholars often describe the Spanish Conquest as having created a legacy of problems for Mexicans, Chicano scholars would see the later conquest as being more significant.

6. Luis Valdez and Stan Steiner, eds., *Aztlán: An Anthology of Mexican American Literature* (New York: Alfred A. Knopf, 1972), xiii, xiv.

7. See David Sánchez, "Chicano Power Explained" (mimeographed booklet), Special Collections, Stanford University Libraries, 1.

8. Enriqueta Longeaux y Vásquez, "Despierten hermanos," *El Grito del Norte,* August 24, 1968, p. 6.

9. Octavio Romano, "The Anthropology and Sociology of the Mexican-American: The Distortion of Mexican-American History," *El Grito* 2 (1968): 13–14.

10. Enriqueta Longeaux y Vásquez, "A nuestros lectores," *El Grito del Norte,* September 15, 1968, p. 2.

11. William Madsen, *The Mexican American in South Texas* (New York: Holt, Rinehart and Winston, 1964), 109.

12. Romano, "Anthropology and Sociology," 14.

13. Carey McWilliams, *North from Mexico: The Spanish-Speaking People of the United States* (New York: Greenwood Press, 1968), as quoted in Romano, "Anthropology and Sociology."

14. Tuck, *Not with the Fist,* 198.

15. Interestingly, Julian Samora was both praised and criticized during this period.

16. Octavio Romano, "The Historical and Intellectual Presence of Mexican Americans," *El Grito* (winter 1969): 32–46.

17. Ibid., 40–44.

18. Ibid., 46.

19. Romano's articles and his publication *El Grito* became required reading for Chicano activists. A Chicano student would have been hard pressed to discuss Chicano identity and history without discussing Romano's work.

20. Editorial, *El Grito* 1, no. 1 (fall 1967): 4.

21. Many liberal scholars, in trying to empathize, often added to the stereotypes by being overly sensitive about Chicano issues to the point of condescension. See Américo Paredes, "On Ethnographic Work among Minority Groups," in *New Directions in Chicano Scholarship,* ed. Raymond Romo and Raymond Paredes (La Jolla, Calif.: Chicano Studies Monograph Series, 1978). See also Octavio Romano, "Minorities, History and Cultural Mystique," *El Grito* 1, no. 1 (1967).

22. It is also because of the scarcity of Anglo-American liberal supporters that the Chicano Movement has not been a major theme explored by Anglo-American academicians. Few Anglo-American activists or scholars ever received training in the struggles of Chicanos for equal rights as many did in the black civil-rights battles. See Renato Rosaldo, Jr., *When Natives Talk Back: Chicano Anthropology Since the Late Sixties,* Renato Rosaldo Lecture Series Monograph 2 (Tucson: Mexican American Studies and Research Center, University of Arizona, 1986), 3–20, for a discussion of the early abandonment of Chicano scholarship by Anglo-American scholars, who were unwilling to face Chicano critique of their work.

23. See Juan Gómez-Quiñones, "Toward a Perspective on Chicano History," *Aztlan* (fall 1971): 1–49.

24. Juan Gómez-Quiñones, "Notes on Periodization, 1900–1965," *Aztlan* (spring 1970): 115–18.

25. See Carlos Muñoz, "Toward A Chicano Perspective of Political Analysis," *Aztlan* (fall 1970).

26. Many of the articles published in these journals were reprinted in numerous community and underground newspapers and magazines and thus became accessible to those communities and campuses where the journals were not available.

27. *Caracol* is in itself a work worthy of study, since it served as a vehicle for many artists and essayists to get started. Everything that was submitted was published, and so it encouraged many to continue to pursue their dreams of writing, drawing, and publishing. Headed by Cecilio Garcia-Camarillo, *Caracol* proved to be the most important popular literary magazine of the Movement.

28. More research has to be conducted on those who rediscovered their ethnicity during the years of the Chicano Movement. Many of these "born-again" Chicanos became the most passionate of all the activists.

29. See Acuña, introduction to *Occupied America,* 1st ed.

30. The other book to appear at about the same time was by Matt S. Meier and Feliciano Rivera, *The Chicanos: A History of Mexican Americans* (New York: Hill and Wang, 1972), which was a milder version popular among Anglo-American historians who chose to include the history of Mexican Americans in their courses. That book never quite gained a place in Chicano Studies.

31. The theory would eventually come under attack from Chicano Marxist scholars for having no class-analysis component. Other mainstream Chicano historians would also question the model. As mentioned above, by the second edition of his *Occupied America* in 1981, Acuña had also rethought his political model and so did not include it. Still, the internal-colony model remains influential even today, much in the same manner that Frederick Jackson Turner's discredited theory on the development of the West remains influential among western historians. For a more in-depth explanation of the internal-colony model, see Mario Barrera, Carlos Muñoz, and Charles Ornelas, "The Barrio as Internal Colony," *Urban Affairs Annual Review* 6 (1972): 465–98; see also Tomas Almaguer, "Toward the Study of Chicano Colonialism," *Aztlan* 2, no. 1 (spring 1971): 7–20.

32. Acuña, *Occupied America,* 3d. ed., chapter 11.

33. For information on Emma Tenayuca and Luisa Moreno, see Carlos Larralde, *Mexican American Movements and Leaders* (Los Alamitos, Calif.: Hwong, 1976); for information on El Congreso de los Pueblos de Habla Español, see M. T. García, *Mexican Americans,* 145–74.

34. Juan Gómez-Quiñones, *Sembradores, Ricardo Flores Magón y el Partido Liberal Mexicano: A Eulogy and Critique* (Los Angeles: Aztlán Publications, Chicano Studies Center, University of California, 1973).

35. Marcienne Rocard, *Children of the Sun,* 213.

36. Ibid.

37. Ibid., 213–15.

38. In the works of the Teatro Campesino, La Raza would win its economic battle; in Nephthali De Leon's plays, the Chicano struggle had the blessings of Che Guevara and other fallen revolutionaries; in Rudy Anaya's novels, all answers came from within the Chicano family; and in Evangelina Vigil's poems, the Chicana won her struggles against Anglo society and Chicano men.

39. Nicolas Kanellos, *Mexican American Theater Then and Now* (Houston: Arte Público Press, 1983), 41–51.

40. Most working-class drama was composed of a series of skits and musical numbers; thus they were called variety shows. See Kanellos, *Mexican American Theater,* 19–40.

41. Kanellos deals with this type of sociological dilemma facing Mexican Americans in his discussion of Chicano theater groups; see *Mexican American Theater,* 35–38.

42. Luis Valdez, "Notes on Chicano Theater," in *Aztlán: An Anthology of Mexican American Literature,* ed. Luis Valdez and Stan Steiner (New York: Alfred A. Knopf, 1972), 353–54.

43. The NFWA had become the United Farmworkers Union, or UFW.

44. The taxonomy or lexicon, as some called it, of the Chicano Movement served a useful purpose for activists seeking to change the way the community perceived itself and Anglo-American society. See Valdez, "Notes on Chicano Theater," 354–59.

45. Carlos Muñoz, *Youth, Identity, Power,* 134–35.

46. Ibid., 191–202.

47. Ibid., 138.

48. Ibid., 192.

49. It is important to note that, unlike today, when many Anglo-American students are "forced" to take these courses because of degree requirements, few Anglo-American students took them when they first became part of the college curriculum.

50. In Kingsville, the Chicano Movement depended on the limited facilities of the ethnic studies program and used students to do much of the campaigning, leafleting, and protest marching.

51. Editorial, *El Grito* 3, no. 3 (spring 1970): 2.

52. Ibid.

53. In Kingsville, La Raza Unida Club sponsored Christmas parties for children, Cinco de Mayo celebrations for the community, lectures series, art exhibits, Tejano music concerts, and Chicano plays.

54. Editorial, *El Gallo,* July 28, 1967, p. 2.

55. Longeaux y Vásquez, "A nuestros lectores," 2.

56. For a discussion of Chicano newspapers, see Stephen Casanova, "La Raza Unida Press," 1986, personal collection of I. M. García.

57. This homogeneity did not spill over into political strategies or even rigid ideologies, but it did provide an image of Chicanos deeply committed to a struggle for liberation.

58. For a discussion of the changes that took place in the American Catholic Church after the activism of the 1960s and 1970s, see Jay P. Dolan and Allan Figueroa Deck, S.J., eds., *Hispanic Catholic Culture in the U.S.: Issues and Concerns* (Notre Dame, Ind.: University of Notre Dame Press, 1994).

59. See "Católicos por la raza," *La Raza* (February 1970).

60. Editorial, *El Grito del Norte,* February 11, 1970, p. 2.

61. César Chávez, "The Mexican Americans and the Church," *El Grito* 2, no. 4 (summer 1968).

62. Navarro, "El Partido," 250–52.

63. Luis Valdez, "The Church and the Chicanos," in *Aztlán: An Anthology of Mexican American Literature,* ed. Luis Valdez and Stan Steiner (New York: Alfred A. Knopf, 1972), 387–88.

64. Leo D. Nieto, "The Chicano Movement and the Churches in the United States," *Perkins Journal* (fall 1975).

65. See "Peregrinación, Penitencia, Revolución," by César Chávez (mimeographed; reprinted in Luis Valdez and Stan Steiner, eds., *Aztlán: An Anthology of Mexican American Literature* [New York: Alfred A. Knopf, 1972], 389–90).

66. See Dolan and Deck, *Hispanic Catholic Culture*, 224–36.

67. See "Jesus Christ as a Revolutionist," *El Grito del Norte*, February 11, 1970.

68. "Day of Triumph in Tierra Amarilla," *El Grito del Norte*, January 1969, p. 7.

69. Arthur Rubel, "The Family," in *Mexican Americans in the United States*, ed. John H. Burman (New York: Shenkman Publishing Co., 1970), 214.

70. William Madsen, *Mexican American*, 20.

71. Gloria Molina de Pick, "Reflexiones sobre el feminismo y la raza," *La Luz* (August 1972): 58.

72. Adaljiza Sosa Riddell, "Chicanas and el Movimiento," *Aztlan* 5, nos. 1 and 2 (1974): 160.

73. Enriqueta Longeaux y Vásquez, "The Woman of La Raza," in *Aztlán: An Anthology of Mexican American Literature*, ed. Luis Valdez and Stan Steiner (New York: Alfred A. Knopf, 1972), 272.

74. Enriqueta Longeaux y Vásquez, "The Women of La Raza," *El Grito del Norte*, July 6, 1969.

75. José Montoya, "La Jefita," in *El Espejo—The Mirror: Selected Mexican American Literature*, ed. Octavio V. Romano (Quinto Sol Publications: 1969).

76. See "Our Feminist Heritage," in Martha P. Cotera's *The Chicana Feminist* (Austin, Tex.: Information Systems Development, 1977), 1–7.

77. Martha Cotera made this statement on September 12, 1994, in Austin, Texas, at a training session for producers and writers of an upcoming Public Broadcasting System special on the Chicano Movement.

78. Enriqueta Longeaux y Vásquez, "Woman of La Raza," 274–77.

79. "La Chicana," *El Grito del Norte*, June 5, 1971, special section.

CHAPTER 3

1. Juan Gómez-Quiñones, *Chicano Politics*, 141–46.

2. Gómez-Quiñones, Mario Barrera, and others argue that Chicano Movement organizations often followed contradictory strategies and failed to maintain any sense of ideological consistency.

3. See "El Plan Espiritual de Aztlán," in *Aztlán: An Anthology of Mexican American Literature*, ed. Luis Valdez and Stan Steiner (New York: Alfred A. Knopf, 1972), 402–6.

4. La Raza Unida Party, the Crusade for Justice, the Alianza, the United Farm Workers, and others depended on adult working-class people for their core support

and their legitimacy. Notwithstanding the number of students, the key question for a Movement organization was, "How many people in the community follow you?"

5. I found this quote in Genaro M. Padilla's "Myths and Comparative Cultural Nationalism: The Ideological Uses of Aztlán," in *Aztlán: Essays on the Chicano Homeland,* ed. Rudolfo A. Anaya and Francisco Lomeli (Albuquerque: University of New Mexico Press, 1989), 113. Padilla provides an excellent basis for a discussion of Chicano mythmaking. In fact, the whole anthology is a must for understanding Chicano mythology.

6. See Romano's discussion of Indianist philosophy in his article, "Historical and Intellectual Presence."

7. M. T. García, "In Search of History," 1–20. His book *Mexican Americans* also has a biographical essay on folklorist Arthur L. Campa, 252–92.

8. M. T. García, "In Search of History," 1–20.

9. Octavio Ignacio Romano, "The Historical and Intellectual Presence of Mexican Americans," in *Voices: Readings from El Grito, 1967–1973* (Berkeley, Calif.: Quinto Sol, 1974), 169. *Indigenismo* is a concept that encompasses the characteristics, thoughts, and "ways" of the Indian south of the U.S. border.

10. Ibid., 170.

11. Mexican intellectuals such as Octavio Paz and Samuel Ramos continually denigrated the indigenous aspect of the Mexican character. See Octavio Paz, *El laberinto de la soledad* (Mexico City: Fondo de Cultura, 1959); and Samuel Ramos, *Profile of Man and Culture in Mexico* (Austin: University of Texas Press, 1972).

12. The 1960s and 1970s were years of much guerrilla activity among the poor peasants and Indians in rural communities of Mexico. Little has been written about this activity, but see Elena Poniatowska, *Massacre in Mexico,* trans. Helen R. Lane (Columbia: University of Missouri Press, 1991), for a short discussion on rebellion in modern Mexico and government reaction.

13. Gonzales, *Yo Soy Joaquín,* 16.

14. See Charles C. Cumberland, *Mexico: The Search for Modernity* (New York: Oxford University Press, 1968), for one of those types of works.

15. See Miguel León-Portilla, ed., *The Broken Spears: The Aztec Account of the Conquest of Mexico* (Boston: Beacon Press, 1962), for an example of the type of books Chicano activists began to use to study the *mestizaje.*

16. See Arnold C. Vento, "Myth, Legend and History of Aztec Origins: The Oral Tradition," *Grito del Sol* 3 (July–September 1976): 103, for an example of this type of myth-making.

17. José Vasconcelos and Manuel Gamio, *Aspects of Mexican Civilization* (Chicago: University of Chicago Press, 1926), 90–102.

18. *Yo Soy Joaquín,* 1.

19. Muñoz, *Youth, Identity, Power,* 15.

20. Ibid., 16.

21. PASSO did seek to move in this direction, but as has been noted, it split the organization. See U.S. Representative Henry B. González's scathing attack on Mexican American reformers supportive of the Chicano Movement in "Race Hate," *Congressional Record,* April 3, 1969: 8590.

22. A large number of the student activists were not fluent either. An attempt at being fluent in Spanish was a sign of one's commitment to La Raza. U.S. Congressman Henry B. González often chided activists who promoted nationalism but could not speak Spanish well. See his "Race Hate," 8590.

23. Mexican American–middle-class bashing became quite common in Chicano activist circles. For an academician's version of this kind of bashing, see Rodolfo Alvarez's article "The Psycho-Historical and Socioeconomic Development of the Chicano Community in the United States," *Social Science Quarterly* 53 (March 1973): 920–42.

24. *Yo Soy Joaquín,* 52.

25. See Armando Rendón's *Chicano Manifesto,* which is a litany of praises for the Mexican American barrio life. See also the novel by Rudolfo A. Anaya, *Bless Me Ultima* (Berkeley, Calif.: Quinto Sol, 1972), which extols the virtues of New Mexican traditions. *Caracol* magazine also had numerous essays and short stories about the superiority of the barrio over Anglo-American neighborhoods.

26. Comments like these, along with numerous jokes at the expense of Mexican Americans, were often repeated by those in the working class, but the tone was less strident and sarcastic. For more on jokes in the Mexican American community, see José R. Reyna, *Raza Humor: Chicano Joke Tradition in Texas* (San Antonio, Tex.: Penca Books, 1980), 17–39.

27. See I. M. García's *United We Win,* chapter 2, "Los Cinco de MAYO," 15–33, for a view of how Chicano activists behaved toward barrio residents while organizing a political movement. See also Shockley's *Chicano Revolt,* 111–49.

28. Muñoz, *Identity, Youth, Power,* 33–38.

29. *Yo Soy Joaquín,* 10.

30. See his poem "Desmadrazgo," in *Canto y Grito Mi Liberación* (El Paso, Tex.: Míctla Publications, 1971).

31. Raul Ruiz, "El Partido de la Raza Unida," *La Raza* 1, no. 7 (1972): 6.

32. See David Montejano, *Anglos and Mexicans in the Making of Texas, 1836–1986* (Austin: University of Texas Press, 1987), for a discussion of the history of South Texas.

33. José Angel Gutiérrez, interview with author, Houston, Tex., June 24, 1988. Some of this information also comes from Emilio Zamora, who at one time served as the director of the ethnic studies center.

34. I did serve as vice president of the Trabajadores Unidos, but only on the insistence of the workers.

35. Here again, however, one of the students served in one of the top positions on request from the community citizens, who believed that the students were better

educated and possibly could work more effectively with the liberal lawyers of the legal office.

36. Although *la gente* could be seen as a neutral term, it has usually been used to refer to working-class people. It is rare to hear a Mexican American refer to a group of middle-class people as *la gente*.

37. Revolutionaries like Che Guevara and Fidel Castro were popular because they were Latinos who had taken on American imperialism and won. See Luis Valdez and Roberto Rubalcava, "Venceremos! Mexican American Statement on Travel to Cuba" (mimeographed; reprinted in *Aztlán: An Anthology of Mexican American Literature,* eds. Luis Valdez and Stan Steiner [New York: Alfred A. Knopf, 1972], 214–18).

38. David L. Torres and Melissa Amado, "The Quest for Power: Hispanic Collective Action in Frontier Arizona," *Perspectives in Mexican American Studies* 3 (1992): 73–94.

39. For a good discussion on internal-community building, see Antonio Ríos-Bustamante, *An Illustrated History of Mexican Los Angeles 1781–1985* (Los Angeles: UCLA Chicano Studies Research Center Publications, 1986). See in particular chapters 5 and 6. See also Thomas E. Sheridan, *Los Tucsonenses: The Mexican Community in Tucson, 1854–1941* (Tucson: University of Arizona Press, 1986), 111–51.

40. José Angel Gutiérrez, interview with author, Houston, Tex., May 24, 1988.

41. I. M. García, *United We Win,* 229–30.

42. For a discussion of challenges to Gutiérrez's power, see Tom Curtis, "Raza Desunida," *Texas Monthly* (February 1977): 102; and "New Worlds or Old Words," *Corpus Christi Caller,* September 22–29, 1975 (a seven-part series).

43. Salomón Baldenegro, interview with author, Tucson, Ariz., summer 1992.

44. Ibid.

45. Ibid.

46. Richard García, in his *Rise of the Mexican American Middle Class: San Antonio 1929–1941,* posits that many in the Mexican American Generation had, by the late 1950s, lost a large part of their sense of community with the working class.

47. Baldenegro, interview, 1992.

48. Ibid.

49. José Reyna, "Tejano Music as an Expression of Cultural Nationalism," *Revista Chicano-Riquena* 4, no. 3 (1976): 37. See also José E. Limon, "Texas Mexican Popular Music and Dancing: Some Notes on History and Symbolic Process," *Latin American Music Review* 4, no. 2 (1983): 229–45. For an example of music produced specifically for the Movement, see Alfredo Zamora, Jr., "Que viva la raza! Que viva la causa! Que viva la revolución!" (mimeographed Chicano song booklet), Ignacio García Movement Collection, Special Collections and Archives, Texas A & M University Library.

50. Manuel Peña, *The Texas-Mexican Conjunto: History of a Working Class Music* (Austin: University of Texas Press, 1985), 8.

51. Ibid., 113–25.

52. Reyna, "Tejano Music as an Expression," 38.

53. José Reyna, "Notes on Tejano Music," *Perspectives in Mexican American Studies* 1 (1988): 40–43.

54. Reyna, "Tejano Music as an Expression," 40.

55. In the case of some songs of the Mexican Revolution, the words were changed to reflect the Chicano experience. For a discussion of the Mexican Revolution and its emotional and psychological impact on the Mexican mind, see Claudio Lomnitz-Adler, *Exits from the Labyrinth: Culture and Ideology in the Mexican National Space* (Berkeley: University of California Press, 1992), 261–81.

56. Organizations such as the Mexican American Legal Defense and Education Fund and the Southwest Voter Registration and Education Fund were extremely successful in their efforts, more so than many Chicano nationalist groups, but they did not directly add to the ideological debate or the cultural renaissance within the community. It should be pointed out, however, that these organizations did direct their efforts toward those in the working-class sectors, who most needed their services. See Juan Vásquez, "Watch Out for Willie Velásquez," *Nuestro* (March 1979): 20–24, for a discussion of the Southwest Voter Registration and Education Project.

57. See M. T. García's chapter entitled "The Politics of Status: The Election of Raymond L. Telles as Mayor of El Paso, 1957," in his *Mexican Americans,* 113–41.

CHAPTER 4

1. For a discussion of this diversity in political thought, see I. M. García, *United We Win,* 98–102, 151–53, 222–26. See also Gómez-Quiñones, *Chicano Politics,* 141–53. For a discussion of barrio politics versus international politics, see an exchange of letters between Tito Lucero of the Crusade for Justice and José Angel Gutiérrez in *El Gallo,* April 1, 1973. See also the November–December 1973 issue of *Para la Gente.*

2. La Raza Unida Party attempted to establish a national organization to direct the Movement, but it quickly unraveled. See I. M. García, *United We Win,* 135–48.

3. See "El Plan de Delano," in *Aztlán: An Anthology of Mexican American Literature,* ed. Luis Valdez and Stan Steiner (New York: Alfred A. Knopf, 1972), 197–200.

4. Ernesto Galarza and the National Farm Labor Union had tried but did so in the more traditional way. See London and Anderson, "Man of Fire," 38–52.

5. "Plan de Delano," 197–200.

6. Hidalgo led the Mexican independence movement, and Juárez led the resistance to the French Intervention in the 1860s and was Mexico's first full-blooded Indian president.

7. "Plan de Delano," 199. See also Luis Valdez, "The Tale of La Raza," in *Chicano: The Beginnings of Bronze Power,* ed. Renato Rosaldo, Gustave L. Seligmann, and Robert A. Calvert (William Morrow & Co., 1974), 55.

8. Chávez, "Peregrinación," 385–87.

9. Liberals flocked to the UFW, and within a few years, Anglo-American lawyers became part of Chávez's inner circle, much to the chagrin of Chicano activists.

10. See Acuña, *Occupied America,* 2d ed., 190–255, for a review of union activity among Mexican Americans in the early part of the twentieth century.

11. This is a quote from "The Dignity of the Farm Worker," in *Aztlán: An Anthology of Mexican American Literature,* ed. Luis Valdez and Stan Steiner (New York: Alfred A. Knopf, 1972), 209.

12. Ibid., 207–208.

13. Ibid.

14. Ibid.

15. Farmworker activists continually talked about the need for people to accept them as contributors to society, not just laborers who would soon be replaced by machines. In a sense they had Mexicanized field labor and now sought only to make the work honorable and economically stable.

16. The "contract" became a symbol of legitimacy. For over a decade, many Chicanos boycotted grapes and lettuce because they were not grown on farms under union contracts. The contract was more than economics, it was acceptance of the farmworkers as human beings.

17. Gonzales, *Yo Soy Joaquín.*

18. Marín, *Spokesman,* 6.

19. Rodolfo Gonzales, "We Demand: Statement of Chicanos of the Southwest in the Poor People's Campaign," *La Raza Yearbook* (September 1968).

20. Marín, *Spokesman,* 11–13.

21. Ibid., 12.

22. I. M. García, *United We Win,* 93–94.

23. Juan Gómez-Quiñones, *Mexican Students por La Raza* (Austin: Relampago Books, 1978), 14–15.

24. Tony Castro, *Chicano Power: The Emergence of Mexican America* (New York: Saturday Review Press/E.P. Dutton, 1974), 130–32. See also Arturo Madrid-Barela, "In Search of the Authentic Pachuco," *Aztlan* 4, no. 1 (1974): 31–57.

25. Rudolfo A. Anaya, "Aztlán: A Homeland Without Boundaries," in *Aztlán: Essays on the Chicano Homeland,* ed. Rudolfo A. Anaya and Francisco Lomeli (Albuquerque: University of New Mexico Press, 1989), 230–41.

26. See Rudolfo A. Anaya and Francisco Lomeli, eds., *Aztlán: Essays on the Chicano Homeland* (Albuquerque: University of New Mexico Press, 1989), for a more complete discussion of the concept of Aztlán.

27. Luis Leal, "In Search of Aztlán," in *Aztlán: Essays on the Chicano Homeland,* ed. Rudolfo A. Anaya and Francisco Lomeli (Albuquerque: University of New Mexico Press, 1989), 13.

28. "Plan Espiritual," 402–6. This document was written by a committee. Two of those who participated in the writing were Alurista, a Chicano poet, and Juan Gómez-Quiñones.

29. Gonzales had no love for the middle class, but being part of it, he knew that there were those like him who would be moved by their concern for their people to join a predominantly working-class movement. The pride of being "Chicano," he hoped, would bring many to the struggle.

30. See Elizabeth Sutherland Martínez and Enriqueta Longeaux y Vásquez, *Viva la Raza! The Struggle of the Mexican American People* (Garden City: Doubleday, 1974), which deals with urban barrios and the efforts of the Crusade for Justice to combat the ills of urbanization in Denver.

31. Historian Mario T. García referred to Gonzales as an anti-intellectual in a conversation I had with him in the spring of 1990 in Albuquerque. It is likely that Gonzales shared much of the populist disdain for city life and liberal politics with those who saw urbanization as stripping away culture and traditions.

32. The concept of the gadfly came from Reies López Tijerina of the Alianza Federal de Pueblos Libres.

33. This was a common phenomenon in many rural and urban communities of the Southwest. Kennedy, who was one of the first Anglo-American politicians to go after the Mexican American vote, would forever be endeared to many Mexican Americans.

34. "Plan Espiritual," 402.

35. See Elizabeth Salas, *Soldaderas in the Mexican Military* (Austin: University of Texas Press, 1990), for a view of the Mexican soldier-woman.

36. See a document written by Juan José Peña, last national president of the National La Raza Unida Party, "Aspects of the Debate on the Chicana Question," May 12, 1981, personal collection of I. M. García.

37. See I. M. García, *United We Win*, p. 256, footnote 10.

38. M. T. García, *Mexican Americans*, 25–61.

39. See Allsup, *American G.I. Forum*, for a discussion of the organization's efforts at reform.

40. See San Miguel, *Take Heed*, for a discussion of legal battles over education.

41. See Alvarez's "Psycho-Historical and Socioeconomic Development," 920–42.

42. Two works on the establishment of the party are I. M. García's *United We Win* and Shockley's *Chicano Revolt in a Texas Town.*

43. La Raza Unida Party was known as *El Partido de la Raza Unida* in Spanish.

44. I. M. García, *United We Win*, xi.

45. For more on the MAYO structure and its inner workings, see Navarro, "El Partido," 32, 557. See also I. M. García's *United We Win*, 15–33.

46. "On the History of LRUP," *Para la Gente*, October 1977, p. 13. This was the official newspaper of La Raza Unida Party, though it came late in the party's development and at times was disguised as simply a Chicano statewide newspaper.

47. Stephen Casanova's unpublished manuscript, "The Movement for Bilingual/Bicultural Education in Texas: School Boycotts and the Mexican American Youth Organization," personal collection of I. M. García.

48. I. M. García, *United We Win*, 53–74.

49. Ibid.

50. José Angel Gutiérrez, "La Raza and Revolution: The Empirical Conditions for Revolution in Four South Texas Counties" (master's thesis, Saint Mary's University, San Antonio, Tex., 1968), 62–63.

51. Ibid.

52. John Muir, "La Raza's Community Farm Plan," *Texas Observer* (October 15, 1976): 1–3; see also "Zavala County Co-Op: Waylaid Again," *Texas Observer* (September 22, 1978): 10–11.

53. My book *United We Win* discusses their strength within Crystal City to only a limited extent but nonetheless shows them as being influential. See pages 229–30. See also Cotera, *Chicana Feminist,* 18–20.

54. Guadalupe Youngblood, interview with author, Robstown, Tex., July 16, 1985.

55. "La Raza Unida," *La Raza* 1, no. 5 (1970): 10–11.

56. Very little has been written on the Brown Berets. A study of the organization is necessary to understand the kind of militancy that will arise in the urban barrios if Chicanos continue to face poverty and police brutality. For what has been written on the Brown Berets, see Muñoz, *Youth, Identity, Power,* 85–86; "The Brown Berets," *La Raza Yearbook* (September 1968); and David Sánchez, "Chicano Power."

57. See *La Raza* 2, no. 5 (1970): 6. It contains an open letter from the Chicano Liberation Front to a number of corporations targeted for sabotage.

58. Organizations such as *Mujeres por La Raza Unida, La Federación de Mujeres del Partido, Hijas de Cuauhtémoc, Mujeres en Lucha, Mujeres Huelgistas,* and others existed throughout the Southwest and Midwest to give Chicanas a chance to be involved as women in the struggle.

59. Enriqueta Longeaux y Vásquez, "The Women of La Raza," *El Grito del Norte,* July 6, 1969, pp. 8–10.

60. Yolanda Alaniz and Megan Cornish, "The Chicano Struggle: A Racial or National Movement?" *Freedom Socialist* (June–August 1988): 14–15.

61. "La Mujer," in *Texas Raza Unida Party: A Political Action Program for the 1970s* (1972), Nettie Lee Benson Latin American Collection, General Libraries, University of Texas at Austin. This was the platform of La Raza Unida Party.

62. Rodolfo "Corky" Gonzales made that comment during a rally. See *La Raza! Why a Chicano Party? Why Chicano Studies?* (New York: Pathfinder Press, 1970), 9.

63. Evey Chapa, "Mujeres por la Raza Unida," *Caracol* 1, no. 2 (October 1974); also, Vicente N. Carranza, "Chicanos and the Future with Raza Unida Party," *Caracol* 3, no. 3 (November 1976): 21.

64. Martha Cotera made this comment during a panel discussion in which I participated, October 1994, Austin, Texas. This panel was part of a training session for writers and producers working on the documentary series *Chicanos: The Mexican American Civil Rights Movement.*

65. Magdalena Mora and Adelaida R. Del Castillo, eds., *Mexican Women in the United States: Struggles Past and Present* (Los Angeles: UCLA Chicano Studies Research Center, 1980). For more on Chicanas and the Movement, see Adaljiza Sosa

Riddell, "Chicanas and el Movimiento," 155–65; Evey Chapa and Armando Gutiérrez, "Chicanas in Politics: An Overview and a Case Study," in *Perspectivas en Chicano Studies I: Proceedings of the Third Annual Meeting of the National Association of
Chicano Social Science,* ed. Reynaldo Flores Macías (Los Angeles: UCLA Chicano
Studies Center, 1975), 137–55; "Mujeres de La Raza Unida," *Echo* 5 (February 1974);
and Alma Zuniga, "Chicanas for the Raza Unida Party," May 9, 1978, personal collection of I. M. García. For a male activist's perception of the Chicana in the Movement,
see Juan José Peña, "Aspects of the Debate on the Chicana Question," May 12, 1981,
personal collection of I. M. García.

66. See Alma M. Garcia, "The Development of Chicana Feminist Discourse,
1970–1980" in *Unequal Sisters,* ed. Ellen Carol Dubois and Vicki L. Ruiz (New York:
Routledge, 1990), 418–31. This essay explains the dichotomy between feminists and
loyalists.

67. Ibid.

68. For a further discussion of CASA, see Gutiérrez, *CASA in the Chicano Move-
ment.* See also "C.A.S.A. General Brotherhood of Workers Salutes National Chicano
Forum" (mimeographed brochure, 1976), CASA Collection, Stanford University
Library; and "Reporte sobre la conferencia nacional sobre imigración y política
pública" (mimeographed minutes from October 28–30 and December 16, 1977),
CASA Collection.

69. See Antonio Ríos-Bustamante, *Mexicans in the United States and the National
Question* (Santa Barbara, Calif.: Editorial La Causa, 1978). See also Tatcho Mindiola,
"Marxism and the Chicano Movement: Preliminary Remarks," in *Perspectivas en
Chicano Studies,* ed. Reynaldo Macías (Los Angeles: UCLA Chicano Studies Center
Publications, 1977), 179–86; and Carlos Vásquez, "National Conference on Immigra-
tion and Public Policy" (mimeographed memo from Carlos Vásquez to all local com-
missions and organizations, October 7, 1977), CASA Collection.

70. For a discussion of Chicano Movement rhetoric, see Hammerback, Jensen,
and Gutiérrez, *War of Words;* see also Robert T. Lee, "Rhetoric of La Raza" (Ph.D.
diss., Arizona State University, 1971).

71. José Angel Gutiérrez, interview with author, Houston, Tex., May 24, 1988.

72. "Raza Unida Nominee Discusses Party Stands," *The Militant* (July 24, 1970):
9. The nominee was Albert Gurulé, candidate for governor in 1970.

73. For more on Kingsville politics, see I. M. García, *United We Win,* 40, 161–64,
203, 221.

74. The Chicano Moratorium was a major Chicano antiwar protest in Los Angeles in 1970. It turned violent, and well-known journalist Ruben Salazar was killed by
police.

CHAPTER 5

1. Driscoll Foundation, "The Driscoll" (undated brochure), Special Collections
and Archives, Texas A & M University, Corpus Christi, pp. 17–20.

2. Robert L. Petersen, "Robert L. Petersen Traces Steps That Led to Founding of City," October 31, 1957, Special Collections and Archives, Texas A & M University, Corpus Christi, p. 3.

3. See David Montejano's *Anglos and Mexicans in the Making of Texas, 1836–1986* (Austin: University of Texas Press, 1987), for an explanation of this agricultural revolution in South Texas.

4. Pamphlet produced for the fiftieth anniversary of Robstown's Lodge 1062, Special Collections and Archives, Texas A & M University, Corpus Christi.

5. David Montejano, *Anglos and Mexicans,* 110–16.

6. C. Edge, "Unpublished History of Robstown," September 27, 1976, Special Collections and Archives, Texas A & M University, Corpus Christi, p. 1.

7. Linda Kohler, interview with author, Corpus Christi, Tex., October 1993. Kohler was a long-time resident of Robstown.

8. Edge, "Unpublished History," p. 1.

9. Not much has been written on this group of people in Robstown or nearby Corpus Christi. Much of this information comes from the papers of Hector P. García (Special Collections and Archives, Texas A & M University, Corpus Christi). We know that there were a number of Mexican Americans elected to office and who held positions of some limited importance even before the Movement arrived in Robstown. For a much wider discussion on ethnic conflicts and some of the early activism in this area, see Paul Taylor, *An American-Mexican Frontier: Nueces County, Texas* (Chapel Hill: University of North Carolina Press, 1934; reprint, New York: Russell & Russell, 1971).

10. Edge, "Unpublished History," p. 2.

11. American G.I. Forum, "School Inspection Report on Fourteen Schools," April 1949, Special Collections and Archives, Texas A & M University, Corpus Christi.

12. "Robstown Latins Suffer Poverty," *Robstown Record,* November 18, 1965, p. 4.

13. The Special Collections and Archives of Texas A & M University, Corpus Christi, has a large collection of the *Robstown Record.* This outstanding archive also has numerous letters, manuscripts, memoirs, and other written materials by Robstown citizens.

14. "La Lomita de la Libertad," *El Grito del Norte,* June 27, 1972.

15. The Hector P. García Collection, which constitutes the major part of the collection of the American G.I. Forum, contains a large number of handwritten reports on segregation in Texas schools.

16. For a study of small-town schools in American society, see Arthur J. Vidich and Joseph Bensman, *Small Town in Mass Society: Class, Power and Religion in a Rural Community* (New Jersey: Princeton University Press, 1968), 171–96.

17. "School Boycott at Robstown Ends after Accord Reached," *Corpus Christi Caller,* April 7, 1972, p. 1.

18. Ibid.

19. Stephen Casanova, "Bilingual/Bicultural Education," 1–6.

20. Youngblood, interview.

21. "Walkout Is Called Today after Meet Ends in Row," *Corpus Christi Caller,* April 11, 1972.

22. "Lomita de la Libertad."

23. Ibid.

24. Youngblood, interview.

25. "Speakers at Robstown Rally Call for Spread of Boycott," *Corpus Christi Caller,* April 30, 1972.

26. "Lomita de la Libertad."

27. Letter to the editor, *Corpus Christi Caller,* December 11, 1974.

28. Abraham Arevalo, "Ni Tuyo Ni Mio," *La Lomita,* December 1972, p. 4.

29. "Lomita de la Libertad."

30. Youngblood, interview.

31. This occurred in 1975. I attended a number of the Robstown rallies and re-member meeting the three Baptist candidates in a backyard rally. They made it a point to tell the crowd that their Mexicanness united them even when their religion divided them.

32. Guadalupe Youngblood was in that situation, and so would be Carlos Guerra after the mid-1970s. There were also a number of others who had attended Texas A & I University nearby and had stayed in Robstown.

33. Gonzales, *Yo Soy Joaquín.*

34. Youngblood, interview.

35. In a less than diplomatic move, members of *Familias Unidas* surrounded the police station and taunted the policemen to come out and be "brutal" with a crowd prepared to confront them. This happened around 1973, according to Guadalupe Youngblood.

36. "Schools in Robstown May Lose Accreditation," *Corpus Christi Caller,* August 27, 1975.

37. Editorial, *La Lomita,* July 1975.

38. "Robstown Feeling Heat of Oncoming Raza Unida Flame," *Corpus Christi Caller,* June 28, 1975.

39. "Unity Party Wins Bout with Familias," *Corpus Christi Caller,* July 1, 1975; see also "Robstown Feeling Heat," *Corpus Christi Caller.*

40. "Robstown Feeling Heat."

41. *Familias Unidas* did win one seat in the school board race but still lost the majority on the board. See "Political Gulf Widens," *Corpus Christi Caller,* May 4, 1976; and "Robstown Trustees Must Certify Returns," *Corpus Christi Caller,* April 19, 1976.

42. "City Elections Spur Rumors in Robstown," *Corpus Christi Caller,* February 21, 1978.

43. "Robstown Feeling Heat."

44. Abel Cavada, conversation with author, Corpus Christi, Tex., March 1994. Cavada and his wife, Viviana Santiago, served as the lawyers for the Robstown

school district in the 1980s. Cavada said he and his wife provided the legal counsel necessary to fire those members of the district from the old groups that had dominated the schools during the years of Familias Unidas.

45. While I was a professor at nearby Texas A & M University in Corpus Christi, I still found young people from Robstown unsure of their identity and their culture. I admit, however, that there were some who came to the university much more self-assured than did those of other communities where the Movement did not play such an important role.

46. One of my students, Melissa González, told me that as of the fall of 1994, the board was deadlocked on who should teach the one course on Mexican American history—an Anglo-American or a Mexican American.

47. A number of them are part of the Mexican American Democrats of Texas, a group that formed shortly before the demise of La Raza Unida Party to represent Chicano interests within the Democratic Party.

CHAPTER 6

1. See Juan Gómez-Quiñones's discussion of student activists in *Mexican Students*.

2. Inez Tovar Hernández, interview with Stephen Casanova, San Antonio, Tex., December 28, 1986.

3. Women have now become an important part of the group of Mexican American elected officials. See "Latinas Want Administration Posts," *Hispanic Link Weekly Report* 11, no. 7 (February 15, 1993): 1.

4. See I. M. García, *United We Win*, 229–31.

5. Ibid., 104–16, 138–40.

6. Acuña, *Occupied America*, 393–94.

7. María Elena Martínez, interview with author, San Antonio, Tex., December 27, 1986. Martínez was one of the last chairpersons of La Raza Unida Party.

8. Chela Sandoval, "U.S. Third World Feminism: The Theory and Method of Oppositional Consciousness in the Postmodern World," *Genders* no. 10 (spring 1991): 1–24.

9. See I. M. García's *United We Win*, 197–232, for a discussion of the decline of La Raza Unida Party and the Movement. Another viewpoint can be found in Gómez-Quiñones's *Chicano Politics*, 141–53.

10. I. M. García, *United We Win*, 219–32; see also José Angel Gutiérrez, *Chicanos and Mexicans under Surveillance: 1940–1980*, Renato Rosaldo Lecture Series Monograph 2 (Tucson: Mexican American Studies and Research Center, University of Arizona, 1986), 27–58.

11. Not much has been written about this effort. For some light on these reformers, see San Miguel's *Take Heed* and Allsup's *American G.I. Forum*.

12. For a discussion of this "postliberalism," see Peter Skerry, *Mexican Americans: The Ambivalent Minority* (New York: Free Press, 1993). Skerry, a conservative

scholar, does not use the term "postliberalism" but presents a detailed review of what he calls "minority" politics. I refer to it as the "politics of ethnicity."

13. For more on this generation, see my article "Backwards from Aztlán: Politics in the Age of Hispanics," in *Chicanos and Chicanas in Contemporary Society*, ed. Roberto De Anda (Boston: Allyson & Baker, 1995), 191–204.

14. Ibid.

15. David T. Abalos, *Latinos in the United States* (Notre Dame, Ind.: University of Notre Dame Press, 1986).

Index

accommodation, 3, 131

Acuña, Rodolfo, 5, 7, 48–51, 57

African Americans, 5, 9, 10, 30, 32

Alianza Federal de Pueblos Libres, 6, 11, 14, 32

Amado, Melissa, 78

American G.I. Forum, 19, 22–23, 40, 81, 100, 119–121

Americanization, 2–21, 76

Anaya, Rudolfo, 95

Anglo Americans: chicano dislike of, 114; circumvention of law by, 29; confrontation with, 68; encroachment of, 47; free of, 12; intimidation of, 103; racism of, 13; shift blame to, 3; similarities with, 10

Arevalo, Abraham, 124

Asociación Nacional Mexico-Americana, 22

August Twenty-third Movement, 107

Aztlán: besieged in, 68; definition of, 18; politics of, 127; symbolic creation of, 95

Aztlán (Journal), 48

Baldenegro, Cecilia, 81–82

Baldenegro, Salomón, 81–82

Barrera, Mario, 5, 7

barrio: control of, 97; image of, 74–76; lack of changes in, 26; problems of, 12; unemployment in, 27

Bonilla, Ruben, 42

Brown Berets, 58, 93, 106–107

Camarillo, Albert, 51

Campa, Arthur L., 70

capitalism, 10, 63, 68, 70

Caracol, 48, 59

Carpas, 53–54

CASA-Hermandad General de Trabajadores, 40, 111–112, 140

Castañeda, Carlos, 70

Castillo, Lupita, 81–82, 138

Castro, Fidel, 52

Castro, Rosie, 137–138

Catholic Church, 61, 78, 88

Chávez, César, 14, 30, 31, 54, 61–62, 88–91

Chávez, Dennis, 23, 29

Chicanas: affected by history, 63–66; in Crystal City, 104; fought traditional roles, 136–139; movement challenged by, 14; movement inclusion of, 15; organizations for, 107–111; role in Aztlán, 98–99

Chicanismo, 6, 8, 14, 87, 94, 105, 108, 114, 141–142

About the Author

Ignacio M. García is an associate professor of history at Brigham Young University in Provo, Utah. He received his Ph.D. from the University of Arizona. His publications include the highly acclaimed book *United We Win: The Rise and Fall of La Raza Unida Party* and articles on Chicano studies and Chicano politics in two recent anthologies: *Chicanas/Chicanos at the Crossroads,* published by the University of Arizona Press, and *Chicanas and Chicanos in Contemporary Society.* His research interests are Chicano political and religious history; his next two projects are a book on the Viva Kennedy clubs of 1960 and a study of Latinos in the Mormon Church.